I NEVER WALK THE HALLS ALONE

I NEVER WALK THE HALLS ALONE

DONNA KINCHELOE
RN, BSN, CCRN

AW PRESS

Cover Design by Eric Walljasper Design
Interior Design by Eric Walljasper Design

Packaged by ACW Press
PO Box 110390
Nashville, TN 37222
www.acwpress.com
The views expressed or implied in this work do not necessarily reflect those of ACW Press. Ultimate design, content, and editorial accuracy of this work is the responsibility of the author(s).

Publisher's Cataloging-in-Publication Data
(Provided by Cassidy Cataloguing Services, Inc.)

Kincheloe, Donna.

   I never walk the halls alone / Donna Kincheloe. -- 1st ed.
Nashville, TN : ACW Press, 2007.

    p. ; cm.
   ISBN: 978-1-932124-90-3

    1. Christian life. 2. Caregivers--Religious life. 3. Medical personnel--Religious life. I. Title.

BV4501.3 .K56 2007
248.4--dc22   0709

Printed in the United States of America.

Contents

Acknowledgments

Thanks to all of the special people God has placed in my life. Those who encourage, love, admonish, and keep me focused on the true meaning of life: honoring God. You know who you are. So glad you share this side of eternity with me.

1. The Private Collection

Come seeking and you're sure to find:
a blessing for your heart and mind,
some comfort for your pain.
Read these words and I will tell
stories that can make you well
God's grace will fall like rain.
Lay down your heartaches and your fears,
Accept His love. Let him draw near.
Your life will never be the same!

Donna Kincheloe

SEVERAL YEARS AGO I attended a Christian writers' conference held at a local church. The speaker's love for Jesus was evident as she incorporated scriptures to emphasize the significance of Christian writing. She also stressed the urgency of writing "in such a time as this" (Esther 4:14). She also emphasized this critical point, "If Christians do not write, the world will."

I left that conference with a burning desire to complete this manuscript posthaste. But life got in the way of my good intentions. It has been close to seven years since I attended that conference, yet I have never forgotten the principles and concepts essential for good writing. Foundational questions must be posed, pondered, and answered by the author such as:

- Why another book?
- Is there a need for another book with this subject or theme?
- Who would want to read this book?

I have considered the above questions. Please examine my rationale.

Why *Another* Book?

Imagine that Sam is a selfish collector of priceless jewelry that he has hoarded for years and kept in a locked chest in the attic. You could say that he is a "selfish collector." Safely tucked away from any other human being, the beauty of the valuable items would never be appreciated or seen by anyone's eyes but Sam's. Then for some reason, Sam experiences a drastic change of heart. He decides to take his precious treasure chest down from its hiding place. He carefully removes each jewel. He displays them in a public place and makes them available to be viewed and enjoyed by any interested party.

Finally removed from the darkness of the chest, the effects of light on the jewels attract curious bystanders as diamond necklaces and bracelets sparkle and the rubies, emeralds and sapphires glow with their deep rich colors. As people approach his table, Sam begins to relay the details and history of the heirlooms he has collected throughout his life. His honesty and willingness to share his stories give special meaning to each gem as his memories and adventures touch the hearts and lives of those he meets.

Just like Sam, I too have a treasure chest. Priceless stories locked up in my heart and memory. I am convinced that the jewels within my personal collection should be made available for anyone to examine and enjoy. I am a Christian. I am a nurse. In my treasure chest are stories that reveal the faithfulness of God present in the lives of precious patients and friends as they experience the mysteries of life and death. Why another book? Because I would never enjoy the title of "selfish collector."

Is There a Need for Another Book with this Subject or Theme?

This question forces the author to pinpoint the main concept of the manuscript. Books have a binding that connects and hold the pages and cover secure. The theme within a book is like an unbreakable cord that ties each chapter and lesson together. The theme of *I Never Walk the Halls Alone* runs parallel to the theme of my favorite reference, the Bible. When a person considers the common thread that ties the sixty-six books together, a variety of themes may be uncovered:

- A loving, Holy God pursuing a relationship with sinful man
- The continual battle between the forces of good and evil
- A book about God
- The salvation of God
- Love

The list could be endless. My personal preference is to examine the theme of the Bible in terms of the word *Life*:

- Creation of life
- The garden life (sinless and sinful)
- Instructions for life
- The life of Christ
- Abundant life
- Eternal life

Life, the Christian Life. This book is definitely about this subject and theme. It contains a multitude of concepts and scriptures from the Bible. For anyone who is unsure of what is meant by the term "Christian life," allow me to provide you with the best explanation I have ever heard.

Years ago, I had the opportunity to hear Major Ian Thomas preach at a church revival. He explained the Christian Life by posing this question: "Who can live the Christian Life?" His answer shocked me, "NO ONE!" I thought the Major had lost his mind. I thought to myself, *If this is true, what in the world have I been doing, claiming to be a Christian all these years? What am I—a fraud?*

Then the Major continued, "No one can live the Christian life. No one can be good enough. No one can try hard enough. No human being can live the Christian Life."

Then he explained his position with a concept that powerfully changed my life forever. "The only person capable of living the Christian Life is CHRIST! You can't; He CAN!"

In order to support his claim, the Major proceeded to provide scriptures that I had known for years. Yet, they seemed to have a whole new meaning:

> To them God has chosen to make known among the Gentiles the glorious riches of this mystery, which is *Christ in You* the hope of glory (Col.1:27, *italics* added).

> I have been crucified with Christ and I no longer live, but *Christ lives in me.* The life I live in the body, I live by faith in the Son of God, who loved me and gave himself for me (Gal. 2:20, *italics* added).

> Since, then, you have been raised with Christ, set your hearts on things above, where Christ is seated at the right hand of God. Set your minds on things above, not on earthly things. For you died and your life is now hidden with Christ in God. When *Christ who is your life* appears then you also will appear with him in glory (Col. 3:1-4, *italics* added).

Christ, living in the Christian, continues to walk this earth using our hands, our hearts, and our feet. Christ touches lives, today, because we are available to Him.

Is there a need for another book with this subject or theme? The answer is definitely yes! If Jesus is living His life within Christians, His interventions and actions are just as significant and precious to believers today as they were centuries ago. In Hebrews 13:8, Scripture verifies the fact that Jesus Christ is the same yesterday, today, and forever. Christ is alive. He is the Living Word. A record of stories that reveal Christ living in and through devoted Christians in our present world is indeed a necessity. Who among us does not need hope, refreshing, and stretching of our faith by the recognition of God and His actions? Do you seriously believe that when the Bible was compiled the faith stories ended? I don't. I believe that Christ continues to write gospel with our lives. I believe that the good news continues, and God's display of His most precious jewels will meet deep needs of many hearts.

Who Would Want to Read this Book?

People seeking a deeper understanding of the salvation Christ provides and through the examination of true faith stories perhaps may consider new ways to apply this knowledge to daily life. Christians who echo David's request from Psalm 51:12 when he wrote, "Restore to me the Joy of your salvation." If you need some joy restoration, you may find yourself renewed, educated, and challenged by this book.

Those who need a reminder that God intervenes in our daily lives. Reading about circumstances that have no other explanation but God, will enhance faith and renew hope. Recognition of His powerful control of our activities and outcomes brings peace and awe to a world that is often filled with confusion and turmoil. If cancer has touched your life or the life of a loved one, you may find a story in this book that contains a word or situation that could give a dying person a precious thought to cling to in the difficult moments. If words don't come easy when speaking to people who are facing a terminal illness, feel free to use the ones you will find tucked in the pages ahead.

Believers and nonbelievers who wonder about the power of prayer may find new perspectives by knowing God's responses to the prayers of others. A sad, young girl asked this question during Sunday school, "Why doesn't God answer prayer today, the way He did in the Bible?" Prayer is a huge subject to ponder. In the following pages are Scripture and true-life examples that touch on the subjects of answered prayer and persistent unanswered prayer.

Christians or non-Christians who are seeking some possible credible rationale when traumatic incidents slam their lives with grief and loss will find some resolve or degree of comfort. Evil is real and it touches and destroys the lives of many. Nurses see it up close and personal. God helps me to cope, and my prayer is that by sharing these coping measures, you will be helped, too.

People trying to deal with the anger, sadness, and frustration produced by harassments, threats, and false accusations. Finding ways to protect your contentment and peace regardless of these distressing circumstances may seem to be the impossible dream. However, we must remember the words of Luke, "For nothing is impossible with God" (Luke 1:37).

Those who work in any area of care-giving including lab workers, nursing assistants, pharmacists, hospital chaplains, nursing staff, social workers, hospice workers, and even family members caring for a loved one at home possess the common bond of caring. This is a special group of men and women who all have a private collection or treasure chest of stories and memories. *I Never Walk the Halls Alone*, provides a glimpse of what we encounter daily.

So, who would want to read this book? This book is intended for anyone seeking salvation, comfort, hope, faith, help, and most importantly, an infusion of Christ Himself. Remember, the Lord said, "You will seek me and find me when you seek me with your whole heart" (Jer. 29:13). He is indeed, the ultimate FIND!

The fundamental questions are answered, and the rationale is complete. The time is now to approach the treasure chest, unlock it, throw back the lid, and disclose the contents of my private collection. Gems are aglow and available for anyone to view and handle. Grandma will simplify the understanding of salvation with her apple pie in "Salvation by the Slice." Enjoy the way God orchestrates life when He is my "Paul Harvey God" and perhaps in your own life, the word *coincidence* will be transformed into *God-incidence*! Ponder the power available to all who pray as you examine "Quality Connections." Your personal prayer life may change drastically, for you may try out the "Stat" line! The truth of "The Whatever Principle" is sure to be of benefit to all who long for that closer walk with Christ Jesus our Savior, no matter how hot the furnace fires. Dare we read the writing on the wall and willingly jump onto the scales secure in the knowledge that "God's Expectations" are connected to his "Promises"? Get ready for life-change. Gratefully don yourself with "God's Gear" as you consider the risks involved with improper attire. Review of "Enemy Tactics" will provide strategic advantages for those enlisted in the army of God. Self-examination results in renewal and hope as we ponder the question, "Are You Looking for a Sign?"

These are the heirlooms, the gold of my life, the priceless treasures of Jesus alive and constantly at work. Hebrews 12:2 identifies Jesus as the "Author and Perfecter" of our faith. May you find whatever precious gems the Lord intends for you to examine, to treasure, and to keep for your very own as you wander through the pages of *I Never Walk the Halls Alone*.

2. Salvation by the Slice

NESTLED IN THE WOODS of Pennsylvania, the little, white Khaletown Church stood proudly on the hilltop. It truly was amazing that every Sunday morning so many people from various faiths and towns would travel the narrow, winding roads that led to this old, non-denominational, country church. Complete with a cemetery, outhouses, and a shelter for reunions and church picnics, these grounds hold a special place in my childhood memories, for this is where my Christian education began.

Jim D. was my Sunday school teacher. When I say *my* teacher, I mean it, for I was usually the only teenager who attended. His worn Bible was the text, King James of course. He probably was the most sincerely devoted man of faith and prayer that I have ever known. He taught me something valuable: commitment. He was there for me each Sunday morning, and it never bothered him that I was the only one in the class. Because he was committed to me, I was committed to him. If I was tired and wished that I could stay home and sleep in, I would think to myself, *If I don't go to church, Jim won't have anyone to teach.* It never dawned on me that Jim might have enjoyed attending the adult Sunday school class. Truth be known, my grandparents would never have let me sleep in anyway!

My grandparents were an integral part of this little church community. When there was a death, Grandpa dug the graves with his friend Schneppy (who owned the backhoe). Each Sunday morning Grandma provided the flower arrangements for both sides of the preacher's podium at the front of the church. Gorgeous bouquets of lilacs, dahlias, peonies, and snapdragons—you name it, we grew it! We lived on five acres of ground, and if a plant produced a flower, you could find it in one of our gardens. Tiny violas to purple delphiniums that stood five to six feet tall would catch the eyes of passersby, and people would stop and ask if they could walk through the amazing array of beauty. We met a lot of people and made a lot of friends because of the flowers.

We spent much time planting, weeding, staking, watering, and loving every bloom, especially on Sunday mornings. We got up at the crack of dawn on Sunday and donned our work clothes. Our day began in the kitchen, making breakfast and lunch simultaneously because Grandma and Grandpa loved to invite people to our home after church for a full course meal that usually included the best homemade pies that only Grandma's hands could prepare. After eating breakfast together and cleaning up the dishes, we would hustle out to the garden and find the perfect collection of flowers for the spectacular floral arrangements. When they were completed, we would jump into the car and rush to the church before anyone else arrived so that we could avoid being seen so shabbily dressed! As we would place the vases on the wobbly wooden stands on each side of the podium, we would examine and adjust the vases several times in order to ensure that the best sides would be facing the congregation. Then we would proceed to rush back home, finalize any meal preparation, assure that there were no dirty dishes in the white porcelain sink, and set the table. We would then quickly wash and dress and rush to the church again, being one of the first to arrive for services. Sunday mornings were exhausting.

Sunday school started at 9:00 A.M. and lasted one hour, followed by the church service in the sanctuary that lasted an eternity. I always sat beside my mischievous sister Patti, who would poke me in the ribs or pinch my arm throughout the service, but particularly near the sermon's end. Pastor would always work up a sweat right before the altar call. Patti's pokes were to assure that I would witness certain disaster. With the pastor's arms a-flailing, Patti always waited with anticipation each week for Pastor to whack one of Grandma Cowan's milk glass vases and baptize the congregation with her Cowan Creation. That scenario would allow the church people to see a side of Grandma that was reserved for the home front! She might lose her religion, right there in the church. Even though the flowers would jiggle and the vases would vibrate with the pastor's furious gestures, the vases never toppled, and the flowers never flew. But weekly under this man's preaching my peace and joy would routinely fall flat on the floor. Every Sunday I was told that I was a horrible sinner. He'd shout, "Satan, like a roaring lion is on a rampage, seeking whom he may devour. He's waiting at this very moment right outside the foyer doors."

Well let him wait, would be my thoughts. *He's not gonna eat me!*

When the altar call came, I would run to the altar and fall on my knees terrified, weeping and wailing. Communion Sunday was even worse. The focus and concentration was on a disease called "sin," and we all had it in a bad way. In my heart I always felt that Pastor would have made a great evangelist in a foreign country. He could have saved a million souls.

I began to wonder how God counts souls that are saved. Personally, I was saved over and over and over again. I knew I was a wretch and a sinner. I suppose that I could have been labeled a professional confessor and repenter. The tragedy was that I attended church every Sunday, yet I did not have any understanding of salvation. Looking back, it seems as though I must have believed that my salvation was contingent upon my confession and constant remorse for my sinful condition. The weekly ritual of going to the altar and crying alligator tears for my sins secured my salvation for that week. That was such wrong thinking!

Years passed. As a young adult, I happened to attend a Christian church on the very night that they were having Communion; it was a Maundy Thursday service. Instinctively, I reached into my purse for Kleenex as the tears began to fall as I thought of what a terrible sinner I was and how I did not deserve Christ. Then the minister said the most bizarre thing that I had ever heard. "We should be so grateful for what Christ has done for us; we should celebrate communion with great joy and overwhelming thanksgiving in our hearts."

What an unbelievable change of focus from what our sins did to Christ to what Christ did with our sins. Then he proceeded to read a scripture that was foreign to me:

"Let us fix our eyes on Jesus, the author and perfecter of our faith, who for the *joy* set before him endured the cross scorning its shame and sat down at the right hand of the throne of God. Consider him who endured such opposition from sinful man, so that you will not grow weary and lose heart" (Heb. 12:2-3, *italics* added).

Joy? Christ endured shame, physical beating, emotional distress, false accusation, and total abandonment by His Father and all those He loved. He not only knew every sin you and I would ever commit, but He was punished because of them. He was able to endure and sustain because of the *joy* set before Him. What thoughts possibly could have flooded His heart and mind that would provide Him with the fortitude to live through this agony? I have come to understand and believe that His thoughts were of you and me and all humanity. He did not dwell on our imperfections; I believe His thoughts were on salvation.

The Holman Bible Dictionary has a strong definition of salvation: "The acutely dynamic act of snatching others by force from serious peril; saving of a life from death or harm."

When Jesus Christ came down from glory to walk upon this earth, He had a specific purpose: saving souls from sin. His purpose was never to throw our sins in our faces and remind us repeatedly of what miserable creatures we are, but He does appreciate and requires that we have a full recognition of our sinful condition. We do need to confess and repent. However, when we continually swim in a pool of despair and cling to the memories of our sinfulness, we can drown in remorse. Christ came to save us from that very depressing state, and He desires that we realize and hold dear to our hearts this most important fact: He is our lifeline, and He rescues us and pulls us out of any pool of sin. Jesus Saves. Jesus alone has possession of salvation. He alone defines it. He alone gives it freely to anyone who desires to be saved. Salvation gives Him great joy, and it should give great joy to anyone who receives it. Often, explaining salvation is complicated and awkward. I wish presenting salvation could be as easy as pie. Maybe it is! Come with me down memory lane to Grandma's tiny kitchen.

Grandma always told me that the way to a man's heart was through his stomach. While in nursing school, I discovered there was no connection whatsoever! Grandma was a magnificent cook, and she taught me so well. Her specialty was her delicious fruit- filled pies. We had an apple orchard behind the house, and she would take her bowl and pick up apples that were ripe and had fallen off the tree. She would wash, peel, core, and slice them; toss them with sugar, cinnamon, and a tad of lemon juice; and set them aside. Preparation of the crust would be the most important task. Flour, shortening, and salt would be worked with her nimble fingers into a fine, cornmeal-like consistency. Using a fork, Grandma would mix the flour crumbs with enough ice water to make a dough ball that would adhere together. Then she would flour a cloth and her trusty wooden rolling pin and ever so gently roll out two crusts. Carefully placing the bottom crust in the pie pan she would dump in the apple filling and dot that with teaspoons of churned butter and cover with the top crust. She would then make some air slits in the top pastry and with her fingers flute the edges perfectly. Grandma would take a bit of milk and dab the crust, and then place the pie in the gas oven at 400 degrees for one hour.

This was Grandma's pie. No one helped her with any part of the process. She invested her time and effort. Her greatest joy? When you would ask her for a piece.

Cutting into the warm, golden, flaky crust, gladly she would place a slice of *her* pie on your plate, hand you a fork and, as you reached out your hands to accept her culinary gift, she would smile and so would you. You asked, you accepted, and you received. Oh, how you appreciate what she has done for you. How sweet it is!

Simply put, Jesus made a marvelous salvation pie without any help from any man or woman. If you'd like a piece, just ask. It is His greatest joy to dish out your portion and watch over you as you enjoy your slice.

"Salvation is found in no one else, for there is no other name under heaven given to men by which we must be saved" (Acts 4:12).

I cannot save myself. Large donations to churches and organizations cannot save me. Nor can frequent trips to the altar. I love to pray on my knees at our church altar, and I do sometimes shed tears. However, I now realize that my salvation is secure, and I no longer need to be saved on a weekly basis. Recently I have come upon a great scripture that addresses this very topic. Jesus Himself says, "My sheep listen to my voice; I know them and they follow me. I give them eternal life and they shall never perish; *no one* can snatch them out of my hand" (John 10:27-28, *italics* added).

Remember the definition of salvation—the acutely dynamic act of snatching others by force from serious peril. I suppose we could say—as long as it is Christ doing the snatching—once snatched, always snatched (and may I add, never devoured by a roaring lion.)

Once a person is saved through faith in Jesus Christ, many transformations take place. In Hebrews 6:9, this statement is made ". . . dear friends we are confident of better things in your case... *things that accompany salvation*" (*italics*, added). The Christian life does not stop when you are saved. You have not arrived; rather, you have only just begun. When you consider all the things that accompany salvation, you could create quite a large list: grace, peace, justification, eternal life, forgiveness, selflessness, etc. The list can go on and on. We have considered *what accompanies* salvation, but let us ponder this question as well, *who* is salvation's companion? The precious Holy Spirit of the Lord Jesus Christ.

Louie, a coal miner, will shine his light on the amazing companion of salvation as he tells the story that changed his life.

Louie's Light

I was working in IV therapy and received a call to the intensive care unit. As I walked into room 3912, sitting up in the bed was a muscular man with hands that were stained and rough from hard, physical labor. Louie was sipping a cup of coffee and, even though he was attached to all kinds of lines, surprisingly he had a look of peace on his face. His red-headed nurse Janie and I exchanged greetings. I received some direction on what she needed from me. Louie needed some antibiotics and new IV site. Then Janie excitedly asked Louie a question. "Oh Louie, could you please tell Donna your story? She would love to hear your story," she pleaded. Janie and I shared a deep love for the Lord, so I was anxious to hear what Louie had to tell me.

"Sure, I'll be happy to. You see I'm a coal miner in an underground mine. Do you know anything about mining?" he inquired.

"Not a thing," I replied honestly.

"Well underground, we always go in teams of two and one works this piece of equipment while one of us works in the back, and a conveyor belt separates the coal. The other day I was working with Brian, and he turned around and could not see my cap light. So, he stopped the machine and came around behind it to find me flat on my back. A huge piece of earth had somehow pinned me to the ground. Brian tried with all of his might to lift it off of me, but I knew he could not do it alone. So I told him to go get the guys from the other teams. So he ran to get help and left me alone. I was laying there in the dark when suddenly there was a bright, white light. I've often heard stories of people having a white light and a tunnel, but there was no tunnel. Just a bright, white light, and there was a presence with me. So I said, 'Lord, if you want to take me, it's all right.' And this is the hard part to explain. I heard a voice, but I did not hear it with my ears; I heard it with my heart, inside me, if that makes any sense at all. The voice said, 'No Louie, you're going to be all right.' About that time the guys showed up and were able to lift that four-hundred-pound chunk of earth off of me enough that I could slide out from under it. Here I am," he smiled. "I have a fractured pelvis, some fractured ribs, and a busted-up wrist."

Then with a more serious tone Louie added, "I have always believed in God, but now… I *know He's real*. And the only question that I have is this, 'Why did He save me?'"

"Oh Louie, I may know the answer to that." I smiled and patted his arm. "You see, you have a story to tell. I bet you work with a lot of tough fellows, and your story will change a lot of lives."

Louie thought about that a minute, shook his head in agreement, and then added, "Well, you know I cuss a lot, but I'm gonna work on that!"

Louie's story shines a light on some very important questions that we all need to ponder. Consider the difference between *believing in a concept* and *knowing a person*. Do you believe *in* God or do you *know* Him? Only when you search your heart for this answer can you understand the meaning of a personal relationship with Christ. A valuable question that Louie asked: Why did Jesus save me?

Why does Jesus save any one of us? If you are saved, what have you done with your "slice of salvation?" Think about these questions in relation to your own salvation and realize that Jesus saved you and loves you tremendously.

One of the most well-known scriptures, and for some the only memorized verse in the Bible, is John 3:16. If you wonder how I came to that conclusion, I suppose you could say that I conducted a small research project. I used to teach Sunday school class for sixth, seventh, and eighth grade students. When I first took this position, I developed a simple questionnaire as a data collection tool in order to assess the knowledge base of the kids in my class. One survey question asked them to write down any memorized Scripture. Out of twenty middle school kids, about a dozen wrote out John 3:16, using various arrangements, paraphrasing, and spellings. The one and only scripture in their memory banks was: "For God so loved the world, that He gave His only begotten Son, that whosoever believeth in Him should not perish but have everlasting life" (KJV).

Why does God save us? Because He loved the world. How does He save us? He sent His one and only son Jesus, who was beaten and crucified on a Roman cross. What exactly does He save us from? SIN! How well do you understand sin? Did you know that sin holds the hand of death? Sin and death are inseparable. A crystal clear picture of sin is found in the following acronym:

S-elfish

I-n

N-ature

When Adam and Eve walked in Eden with God, they were focused on pleasing Him, loving Him, and living life beside Him. Their God had only one restriction for them to observe: "And the Lord God commanded the man, 'You are free to eat from any tree in the garden: but you must not eat from the tree of the knowledge of good and evil for when you eat of it *you will surely die*'" (Gen. 2:16-17, *italics* added).

Then Satan appeared and tempted Eve, twisting God's command. "Did God really say, 'You must not eat from any tree in the Garden?'"

The woman said to the serpent, "We may eat fruit from the trees in the garden, but God did say, 'You must not eat fruit from the tree that is in the middle of the garden, and you must not touch it or you will die.'"
"You will not surely die," the serpent said to the woman.
"For God knows that when you eat of it your eyes will be open and you will be like God, knowing good and evil" (Gen. 3:1-5)

When we evaluate that story, I believe we sometimes overlook the actual temptation presented by Satan. What was the irresistible appeal that made Eve take a piece of fruit from the forbidden tree and share it with Adam? Perhaps it was the thought that man could stand on equal ground with God. Satan's lies have never changed through the years. Beware of his favorite tactic ". . . you, too, can be like God." He has been singing that song since his garden debut. There is one huge catch if you sing along with Beelzebub.

You see our Lord is very specific about His place in the world. "I am the Lord and there is no other. I am the Lord and there is none like me" (Isa. 46:9).

Doesn't His proclamation create a bit of wonder and a great respect when you read those words? He is also extremely comfortable with the position of man in relation to Himself. "Thou shalt have no other gods before me" (Deut. 4:7 KJV).

He is God. He is the one on the throne, and it is a one seat-er! We must recognize that He desires us to be aware that nothing in our lives can be allowed to replace or erase Him. Nothing can come before Him. He gets first billing. So when Adam and Eve ate the fruit, a drastic change occurred on the stage of life.

Exit a perfect relationship and proper standing between man and God.

Enter sin (the garden gift), a condition of man where we turn our back on God, turn our ear to Satan, and pursue a life which is directed by selfish desires, arrogance, and pride.

Sin usually is associated with some type of sensory deficit. Deafness or visual disturbances usually occur when sin is present in our life. Have you ever attended a theater or seen a musical or play and unknowingly find that you have strategically positioned yourself behind a row of very tall people? They block your view. You can't see the show. When the star appears you have a tremendous blind spot. You could not identify or recognize him, because you cannot see him!

Sin blocks your view. Sin is anyone or anything that comes between you and God. Sin is anyone or anything that has your complete attention and unwavering devotion. *Whatever captivates your mind, steals away your time, or hides the fact that you are blind, is sin.*

Distorted focus and tunnel vision are also symptoms of sin. When your eyes refuse to even glance God's way because they are so focused on self, this is a sign of what can only be described as "ME-itis." In the health care arena the suffix "itis" is used to describe inflammation. For example, tonsillitis is the inflammation of the tonsils. Appendicitis is inflammation of the appendix. So it follows that "ME-itis" is the inflammation of self. It is a serious and deadly condition that is manifested by a tremendously enlarged ego, narcissistic attitudes, and total absence of sensitivity or compassion. Favorite words and phrases include: my dreams, my goals, my accomplishments, my success, my wealth, my appearance, and my life. Conversation usually centers on me, me, me.

How do you think God feels about the things that keep us so far from Him? When obstacles in life block our view of God, it must break His heart. Can we begin to imagine His feelings when we choose to love ourselves more than we love Him? I believe that He hates the distant relationship that sin creates. Sin is just as real today as it was in Eden, and we must acknowledge it can take up residence in any human heart.

The garden scenario is often referred to as the Fall of Man or the story of original sin. It is often difficult to connect the events in the garden to our present sinful state. As a nurse, it seems natural to examine the subject of sin by using a parallel with our physical body. Perhaps this illustration will provide an easy way to explain the sinful nature of humankind and God's plan of divine intervention.

Each of us is born with genetic material that is passed down from generation to generation. Certain disease processes are handed down in family lines just like bone structures or eye and hair color. Your family may tell you, "You have Uncle Joe's nose," or maybe you are mechanically inclined, "Just like your grandpa." Adam and Eve sinned and when they did, they did not die physically; instead they suffered a spiritual death. By their disobedience, they contaminated our spiritual blood supply. Every one of us born, since Adam and Eve fell from God's perfect standing, has sin flowing freely through our veins.

A major problem that cannot be ignored is that sin does not stand alone. Sin has an ugly companion or a fatal prognosis: *death*. May I repeat, not physical death, but spiritual death that can be defined as eternal separation from God.

God is holy. He cannot look upon sin. We have contracted a disease that is totally disgusting to our Heavenly Father. Seems like a very hopeless situation, doesn't it? If only we could start over. If only we could find a pure, uncontaminated spiritual blood supply, we could get a transfusion. That may help a bit, but it would not truly take care of this disease. God knew the problem, and He had a solution all along. When Adam and Eve "fell" in the garden, He held the safety net. His plan: to provide the world with a blood transfusion. He would provide a person who would have pure, untainted, spotless blood, and God would perform a transfusion exchange. Anyone willing to come to the blood drive could have their contaminated blood removed and, in exchange, they would receive a totally pure blood transfusion that would save their life and restore their relationship with the Holy Father that was lost in Eden.

Whose blood would meet the sinless requirement? Only one person since Adam sinned has been born without sin and that person happens to be God's only Son. So God sent His Son, and Christ came and gave His blood and took our contaminated, worthless supply. Christ who knew no sin, became sin. Remember, sin is connected to death. Thus Christ took our sin in His own body and died upon that cross. He paid the price, satisfied His Father, and saved us from spiritual death. His obedience removed all the obstacles that obscured our view. We can clearly see God. We can identify His heart and actions in our lives. We no longer have a hopeless, fatal disease. Just cherish the following scripture passage from 2 Corinthians 5:14-21:

> For Christ's love compels us, because we are convinced that one died for all, and therefore all died. And he died for all that those who live should no longer live for themselves *[say goodbye to ME-ism]* but for him who died for them and was raised

again. So from now on we regard no one from a worldly point of view *[our eye sight is clearly focused!]*. Though we once regarded Christ in this way, we do so no longer. Therefore, if anyone is in Christ, he is a new creation; the old has gone, and the new has come! All this is from God, who reconciled us to himself through Christ and gave us the ministry of reconciliation: that God was reconciling the world to himself in Christ *[God restored the relationship lost in Eden!]*, not counting men's sins against them. And he has committed to us the message of reconciliation. We are therefore Christ's ambassadors, as though God were making his appeal through us. We implore you on Christ's behalf: Be reconciled to God. God made him, who had no sin to be sin for us, so that in him we might become the righteousness of God.

Each Christian has a personal journey of walking in faith with Jesus. My beginnings include these memories: my sister's pinching fingers, Pastor's flailing arms and vibrating milk glass vases of garden flowers, Grandma's delicious apple pie, and the devil's insatiable hunger for teenagers. Yet, God never left me dwelling in the sadness and guilt produced from my misconceptions of His salvation. He has taught me His definitions and purposes for life through the lives of those He has connected to mine. I know Him better, for I have asked Him Louie's question, "Lord, why did you save me?" And I believe His answer is evident, "Because I love you." Realize the love that God has for you. Claim it. Treasure it.

Sin. Saved. Snatched. How then shall we live? Enjoying our "Slice of Salvation," knowing we are secure in His love, saved by His blood, and living each day with the confidence that we never walk alone.

3. My Paul Harvey God

HAVE YOU EVER EXPERIENCED the overwhelming love of God so close that you feel His strong arms gently holding you? Have you memories of those extraordinary moments when He has "let you know" things that only He could reveal? Some people might say that these situations occurred by coincidence. However, I choose to believe that God and only God carefully orchestrated the events that took place in each and every case.

Nurses have a tendency to be outcome-driven. We live by a process which includes detailed assessments, care plans, actions, and evaluations and outcomes. Measuring outcomes provides a picture of what we do well and what areas may need improvement. Just like a scale, we can measure specific factors, such as patient satisfaction, infection rates, retention of staff, etc. There is something comforting about knowing the outcome.

When God lets me know the outcome of a situation, I am never more confident of His great love for me. Paul Harvey uses vignettes in his radio talk show. At the beginning of his program, he provides a portion of an adventure or event. Then he leaves his listeners hanging for the entirety of the show until right before the end of his broadcast he makes this statement, "Now for the rest of the story!" God is my "Paul Harvey God" when He lets me know the rest of the story.

The Meltdown

I was working as an IV nurse and was called to the fifth floor to restart an IV on a young woman in her early forties. As I was about to enter the patient's room, I heard a woman sobbing in the bathroom to my left.

I inquired softly, "Are you alright?"

Her response was, "NO! I'm having a meltdown."

Then I simply asked, "Do you need a hug?"

"Yes, I could use one."

I held this dear lady, and miraculously I also held my tongue. Through tears and sobs, she tenderly told me her story.

"You see, that is my daughter in the bed and she is dying of a brain tumor. She has three wonderful children and a husband that loves her deeply. And the worst thing is… she doesn't know she's dying."

Being a nurse who prays a lot, I sent up a silent "stat" prayer from my heart that went like this, "Father, please give me the words to comfort this woman."

And He did. Pondering if this dear one would be receptive to God's words, I asked her a very unarming question. "Are you a woman of faith?"

Her answer was a very definite, "Oh, yes I am." That response gave me the clearance I needed to continue.

"I have something to tell you that may seem very strange to you, but I'm going to tell you anyway." I hesitated for a moment, took in a deep breath and then slowly explained the message.

"This is a picture of God's grace. You see, I only have one son, and if I knew that I was going to die and I had to leave him, it would tear me up. God is sparing your daughter that pain, and you are carrying it instead. You are bearing a heartache that she never has to bear. This is intercessory pain and tears, and it is God's grace to your daughter."

After a bit of mopping up our faces, this precious mother and I walked into the room. I was able to meet this sweet, confused young woman and restart her IV site. I never saw her again during her hospitalization. But one day I ran into her mother.

It was during Christmas time, and I was checking IV sites. I walked into this woman's room and as I was leaving the patient called out, "Wait a minute! I think I know you. You may not remember me, but we met in a bathroom on the fifth floor. I had been crying."

I stopped in my tracks and turned around in disbelief.

"Oh, of course I remember. You were having a meltdown. I will never forget that day," I assured her as I sat down in the chair beside her bed.

"I have so much to tell you," she began. "My daughter had a lovely death. Hospice was wonderful. Her husband and children are doing well. The children get off the bus after school at my house every night. I cannot tell you how many times I have thought about what you told me in that bathroom that day. It helped me get through so much. I have wanted to thank you a million times, but I never even knew your name."

The Rest of the Story: God let me know that the words that He provided in that bathroom that day, gave great comfort to a grieving heart. She didn't remember my name, but I promise you that she will never forget God's interpretation of grace. Make yourself available to God and stand utterly amazed at what He can do. This is the *wow* of God to me. I love knowing *the rest of the story* because I am fully aware that this knowledge is a gift from God to me. He doesn't have to share outcomes with me. He doesn't have to let me know anything. But He knows me so well. He knows my response to His revealing of events is an overwhelming acknowledgement of how much love He has for me.

One spring, He arranged another 'Paul Harvey" situation that brought memories, tears, and closure.

Kicked in the Chest

I had the privilege of attending a marvelous Christian retreat back in 1995. I have since enjoyed working on a number of retreats as a team member serving in various positions. Preparation for a retreat is quite intensive, requiring many meetings prior to the actual retreat weekend. I received a call from the lay director asking me to jump in at the last minute for one of the team members had to drop out. I was happy to help out and spend Thursday through Sunday with forty Christian team members and thirty-eight Christian women. Women attending the weekend were called pilgrims.

Thursday came and went without a hitch. Friday was going great. As I was talking with one of the musicians at the front of the conference room during a break, one of the pilgrims approached me with a big smile on her face.

"I finally figured out where I know you from," she began. "You looked so familiar to me, and I have been asking people if they knew where you worked, and when they told me you were a nurse I remembered. You were my husband's nurse a couple years ago. You took care of my husband Roger."

I have been a nurse for so long that I never get embarrassed asking people for memory assistance. So I jokingly said, "Well, I've taken care of a few patients since then. Can you help me out here a little?"

"Roger was kicked in the chest by a horse," was her reply.

The amazing thing about memories is the degree of emotion they can produce regardless of their age. I threw my arms around this woman's neck, and I began to cry.

"Oh no, I am so sorry. I am so sorry. . . ."

This gem of my nursing career has extremely sharp edges and a very clear stone. It was early, my first page on my beeper. I remember arriving with my IV supply cart to the room on the fourth floor. The patient was a tan, muscular man in his forties and he did not look good. He did not have good color, and he did not have any palpable veins. As I spoke to the man and his wife, I learned that he had been kicked in the chest by a horse, and I became more and more concerned. I called the nurse to inquire why he did not have an IV site, and the answer was that he was a difficult stick and two days before the physician had written the order to leave the IV out. The patient had been stable up until this morning. I asked the RN, "Has anyone taken a blood pressure lately?"

As the staff scurried about getting a set of vital signs, I continued to search for a vein. I looked for every possible site— hands, wrist, cephalic vein, basilic vein, antecubital, and upper arm. Nothing. Absolutely nothing. I looked for the saphenous vein or a foot shot. Nothing. I was earnestly praying under my breath, "Lord Jesus, please help me, I can't find a vein." His blood pressure was extremely low. Critical care nurses are part bulldog so, I instinctively began to gently bark sincere, specific instructions to the staff nurses on the scene, "You need to call his physician stat! He needs to go to ICU, tell him that this man needs a central line placed now." I apologized to the wife and the patient. I was not able to land a site on a very critical patient, and I felt like such a failure.

About two hours later a Code Blue was called in the ICU. It was Roger. As the IV nurse, I responded to the code only to find out that the physicians could not get a central line in this young man either. This man died, and at the time of his death no one knew why. I was crushed.

This precious woman attending this Christian retreat remembered me all right; she had met me once before in her life. The very day her husband died.

"Kelly, I am so sorry I could not save your husband. I could not get a line and I am so sorry," I blubbered. Of all the responses this woman could possibly give to me at that moment, the one she gave left me absolutely dumbfounded.

"Oh, but you helped me so much that day."

What? I wondered if I heard her right. What an unbelievable comment! All I could get out in response was a squeaky, puzzled, "How?"

Through tears she explained, "You are the only one who saw what I saw. You came in that room and took charge. You got things done. You helped me so much."

The break was over and we had to continue with the retreat schedule. Friday evening ended with prayers in the chapel. As Kelly was about to go out the chapel doors, I asked her, "Do you think that we could talk just a little bit more; I haven't cried enough."

So everyone exited the chapel but Kelly, me, and two of the clergy. We sat on the floor in front of the altar, and Kelly told us stories of her life with Roger and her life without him. God let me know how Roger died. Kelly said, "It was really odd, the coroner himself called me at home to tell me that Roger had died from a chest full of blood." I asked Kelly how long it took the nurses to get him to the ICU and she told me, just minutes after you left the room." I shared with her what I remembered about him. He kept on telling her how much he loved her. He kept on encouraging her and expressing his love for her. There was a great deal of healing in that chapel that night, healing for Kelly and healing for me as well.

God let both of us know the rest of the story. On the worst day of her life, God had placed a Christian nurse in her path so that Kelly was covered in prayer and God wanted her to know. I prayed for her and her family for months after that day. One of the greatest things for me was the realization that when I cannot accomplish the task set before me, I should not label myself as a failure. Some tasks are beyond us and our motives, presence, and sincere attempts are noticed, needed, and appreciated. Consider God's divine strategy in this situation. I was a last-minute add-on to the team. No one but God knew of the connection between Kelly and me. He brought the two of us together so that we both would know how much He cares about our deepest hurts, for He alone is the Great Physician and healer. Kelly has completed the course from the bereavement academy and her life of loss has become a life filled with a desire to help others through the grief process. Once again I am blessed to know the rest of the story, so is Kelly.

Soft Spots

I believe that most people have a soft spot—the area of the heart that is vulnerable to extreme pain and distress. My soft spot happens to be child abuse. One evening while working as an IV nurse, I encountered two consecutive families who had lost grandchildren to abuse and murder.

I walked into Charlie's room, introduced myself, and explained that I was there to start his IV. We had such a pleasant conversation. He spoke about his love for music and playing the banjo with his friends throughout the years. Then, as if someone flipped an invisible switch, this happy, fun-loving, seventy-year-old musician, was transformed into a broken man being consumed by such excruciating pain that his body shook uncontrollably, and his loud sobs and cries broke my heart.

"Charlie, what is it? Are you okay?" I asked.

"No! No!" he anguished as the tears streamed down his face, "I will never be okay again. Did you hear about the feller that went out on that lake and drown his little boy?"

"No, Charlie, I don't know about that. What happened?"

"Well, that was my son," he continued, and I remember thinking that the pain in this man's heart was worse than any physical chest pain I have ever witnessed.

Charlie began again, "Well, that was my son. He took his own baby boy out on that boat and held him under the water. Little Ben kept crying, 'Daddy, help me, please help me! Daddy save me! Please save me!'

Blanketed in grief and disbelief Charlie began to call out to God. "Oh God, why, oh why? My grandson is dead. My son is in jail. I asked my son why he did this terrible thing. He told me that the world was evil, and Ben was such a sweet innocent child he did not want him to have to live in such an evil place as this."

Charlie's story was only the beginning of trauma to my soft spot.

The very next room I entered, I met a dear woman whose husband was recuperating from surgery. As I restarted this man's IV site, the patient's wife and I chatted quietly. He was still somewhat sedated from his anesthetics and pain medicines. She was so very proud of her grandchildren; she proceeded to provide me with a photo show of all those precious babes she loved so much. Then she showed me the picture of Michael. This toddler had thick, blonde hair and mischievous bright blue eyes and his smile was sure to light up any room.

"Oh I bet he's a ball of fire," I exclaimed.

"Oh yes, he was… " her voice faded as she took a deep breath and sighed.

Her next question pierced my soft spot.

"Have you ever heard of Shaken Baby Syndrome?" This loving grandmother told me the tragic events that led to the death of this child. Her daughter had been living with a man who had a violent temper. He was a drinker and had zero tolerance for disobedience or crying. In anger, he took hold of this toddler and shook him so violently that the child became limp and unconscious, never to take another breath, let alone whimper or cry.

My silent prayer was simple. "Oh, Father, not another one! Lord

Jesus, You know that I cannot bear this. Why on earth do I have to know about these children? I cannot bear child abuse. These stories make me a basket case. What earthly good can I be to You if I am an emotional wreck? I don't understand why I have to be exposed to all this pain. Why are You doing this to me?"

After washing my face in the privacy of my office, I pondered what benefit knowing about these painful situations could ever produce in my life. I began to imagine child abuse from God's perspective. This thought came to me—if this breaks my heart just *hearing* what happened to these babies, I cannot begin to fathom the depth of pain produced within the heart of God. Reality hit me hard that night. God *sees* it all take place. He sees the beating, the drowning, and the shaking. God hears the little voices crying out for help. Child abuse pains the very heart of God.

Imagine God experiencing heartache. We know that He does. When Jesus walked upon this earth, He was the manifestation of His Holy Father. Remember His heartbreaking experiences? When I read about Jesus having pain on this earth, I often wish that I could have been with Him. Especially this night:

> Then Jesus went with his disciples to a place called Gethsemane, and he said to them, "Sit here while I go over there and pray." He took Peter and the two sons of Zebedee along with him and he began to be sorrowful and troubled. Then he said to them, "My soul is overwhelmed with sorrow to the point of death. Stay here and keep watch with me" (Matt. 26:36-38).

And the disciples could not stay awake. Jesus spent his night of anguish alone.

As His disciple, I want to stay awake with Him. I want to share His pain and His heartaches as well as His victories and joys. I want to cry with my Jesus. I believe that He doesn't want to witness abusive situations anymore than I want to hear about the few that I have been exposed to. He sees them all. As His disciples, we should not ignore the fact that evil things take place in our world. I believe that we would all like very much to bury our heads in ignorance and denial in order to protect the soft spots in our hearts. We would rather sleep, than stay awake and endure pain and suffering. Yet if you make your life available to God, He will reveal your soft spots, illuminate your understanding, and be right beside you as you are covered in pain and sorrow. Could it be possible that when Christians are heartbroken so is CHRIST? If we are awake, He is not alone. This concept broadens the meaning of sharing one another's burdens. It embraces the burdens of our Savior and by doing so, places an intense responsibility upon believers. So often we are so self-absorbed. When God reveals to you the very soft spot of your heart, He is giving you the opportunity to allow Him to reveal situations to you that need your intervention and your prayers.

Personally, as far as I was concerned, I had received quite a life lesson about child abuse, and I was content to tackle another subject matter. However, when God is your teacher, I can promise you that He will not skim over the material, but will provide the deepest interpretations and rationale a human mind can consider. Thus my course in child abuse continued.

Baby Blue Eyes

When I was working in IV therapy, my co-worker Bob was diagnosed with cancer and, in order to help staff the hospital safely, several of us took turns working stretches of night shifts (11:00 P.M. to 7:00 A.M.). On the last night of a seven-night stretch, I received a call to emergency room 7. Our ER was extremely efficient, and room 7 was always reserved for the very worst trauma, heart attack, or car accident. It was 4:00 A.M. when I hurried to ER, totally ignorant of the critical situation that would be rushing through the door at any moment. I talked with the respiratory therapist and other team members as I cut my tape and gathered all my necessary equipment. Suddenly the EMTs rushed through the door. Strapped to the adult ambulance stretcher, in a sitting position was the most precious baby girl with dark, curly hair. She never made a sound. I thought to myself, "What is wrong with this picture?" She had the most penetrating deep, blue eyes. The oxygen mask was way too big for her tiny, little face.

As they moved her over onto the ER gurney, I noticed the bruises on both sides of her little head. My gut knew there was something terribly wrong, while the nurse in me took over. I did a quick visual head to toe inspection and when my eyes examined her chubby legs, I began to feel sick and my hands began to shake. Fresh bruises on her tender skin told the reason for her admission. Someone in a rage took hold of this child. We later found out from the police officers the identity of the man responsible. The bruises on her calves were a perfect match to the hands and fingers of the one who should have loved and protected this life with his own. This father had grabbed his own baby by her legs and smashed her head against a wall.

My hands were shaking uncontrollably. I had everything ready to start this baby's IV, and I got to the task as quickly as I could. The teenage mother and grandmother were crying and holding each other on the left side of the gurney while the ER nurse, Julie, stood behind me documenting information. The moment that my IV needle pierced this baby's skin, she began to have a seizure. Not wanting to alarm the mother and grandmother, I tried to get Julie's attention.

"Julie, Julie, Julie," I repeated softly and quickly.

Her response in an aggravated tone was, "Donna, what do you want?"

With a quiet but emergent tone I quickly retorted, "Would you please look at this child!"

Julie took one look and began to scream loudly for the doctor. In came a crew of EMTs, physicians, and nurses, and when they took in the scene, one nurse ushered the family out of the room.

I had to find another site for this baby's IV. The minute she began to seize I had to remove my needle in order not to harm her. I will never forget the kindness of the EMT who asked, "Donna, what can I do to help you?"

My answer was simple, "If you could just hold my hand still, that would be great." By God's grace I was able to secure a good site for the team to help this baby with anticonvulsant medicines. As I exited the ER, I had a tremendous amount of anger and hate in my heart. Before the family had arrived, the police officers and EMTs were so angry. They expressed their feelings openly. "Whoever did this to this child deserves to die."

I must confess that what went through my mind was even worse. I decided how the abuser should die. My anger was beyond the boiling point; I was totally exhausted and emotionally drained. But I did tell my God exactly how I felt. "Lord, You know the only true justice in a case like this would be to construct a machine and put the one that did this into a vice that would grip him by the legs and smash his head against a wall a couple of times. Only *that* would be justice!"

God not only heard me, but He answered me. The wee small voice of God spoke calmly to my angry heart. "Donna, I died for him too."

Do you remember the Old Testament story of Elijah? It has always been one of my favorites. Elijah felt he was the only one who had remained faithful to God. He was in a state of self-righteousness.

"Then a great and powerful wind tore the mountains apart and shattered the rocks before the Lord, but the Lord was not in the wind. After the wind there was an earthquake, but the Lord was not in the earthquake. After the earthquake came a fire, but the Lord was not in the fire. And after the fire came a gentle whisper. When Elijah heard it, he pulled his cloak over his face and went out and stood at the mouth of the cave" (1 Kings 19:11).

The still, small voice of God brought the prophet back into proper focus. God whispered truth to my heart, and I heard Him clearly. If I believe that God forgives every bruise and mark on Jesus' body that *my sin* attributed to His suffering, I must believe that He bore scars for the child abusers in this world, too. If this man asks for forgiveness, he gets it with as much love and compassion as the Savior offers to all.

Jesus Christ does not rank sin, man does. Sin is sin. Genuine repentance yields undeniable, limitless forgiveness regardless. Driving home from the hospital that morning, I cried for that baby girl. I did not know if she would survive this abuse. I asked God to please take her home to be with him in the event that she would have to spend her life in an abusive situation. I asked God to have mercy and take her to heaven to be with Him if she would have to have a life of tremendous physical pain. I had nightmares about this wee one. I had several days off and when I returned to work I never was able to find out if that baby had lived or died. But remember, my heavenly Father is often, my "Paul Harvey" God.

Fall came. I was attending an English Composition class on Saturday mornings at 8:00. I was working on my bachelor's degree in Nursing. There were only twelve in the class, and we were all nontraditional, adult students working on a variety of degrees. Throughout the course we often would pair up and critique, read, and help each other rewrite any part of our papers. We worked together in different groups each week perfecting the outlines, introductions, bodies, and conclusions of our papers. The morning we were to hand in the final product, I asked the professor, "We have helped each other with our papers for several weeks now. Could we hear the final products?" I felt as though we had gone through the labor process together, and I wanted to see the baby.

His response was, "Sure, anyone interested?"

A student named George sitting in the front of the class jumped to his feet exclaiming, "I'd love to read my paper." He made his way to the podium. Funny thing, I never had the opportunity to pair up with George all through the weeks of preparation. I had no idea what his topic covered.

George began, "The title of my paper is, "Why I am a Christian." He hesitated a moment and then presented his introduction.

"If I were not a Christian, I would be in prison for murder, for the night that my son-in-law took my granddaughter by the legs and bashed her head against a wall. . . ."

My tears flowed, as my mind went back to the previous Saturday. I had met George on the sidewalk; he was on his way to the parking lot, and I was on my way to class. Our professor always told us we could miss any class as long as we brought in our assigned work. George had delivered his assignment and was going to spend the day with his darling granddaughter. In his arms was the most beautiful little girl. She wore a bright yellow jacket, and the wind was blowing her black curls all over her face. I reached up and carefully tucked her curly locks under her hood. Unknowingly, I was touching the sweet face of the very one I had met so many months before in room 7 on that dreadful morning.

George continued reading his paper and God, once again, let me know the rest of the story. The baby girl is developmentally sound. She is totally blind. Her father is in prison. She has Christians in her life. She survived. She is alive. Only God could place me in an English class with

George. Only God would spur me on to ask permission to read our papers. Only God would give George the courage to share his boldly. Only God, can complete the work that is so needed for our soft spots. Only God, can let me know the rest of the story, whenever he chooses.

"I am God, and there is no other; I am God, and there is none like me" (Isa. 46:9).

I am so thankful He is my God. I stand in awe of the waves of love my God throws my way when He exposes my soft spots in order to strengthen my faith, sharpen my focus, and open the eyes of my heart that I may see His divine intervention in my life and in the lives of the Christians around me. May we all be amazed when God lets us know the rest of the story. He truly is our most precious, omnipotent, "Paul Harvey God."

4. Quality Connections

WHEN WE THINK ABOUT the abilities of God, consider the fact that we are so fortunate to worship a Lord who possesses keen senses. He can see, and He can hear. I am very much aware of His power to listen to prayers and the hearts of His people. Perhaps in heaven the actual process of how He hears all who call upon His name will be revealed. However, I am confident that "His arm is not too short, nor is his ear too heavy that he can not hear" (Isa. 59:1 KJV). What comfort to believe that we are never out of His reach nor are we ever speaking to a God who turns a deaf ear.

Do You Believe God Hears You when You Pray?

I received a page to ER, and as soon as I came through the doors I saw her. Cindy was so down she was mopping the floor with her face! One of our best ER nurses, Cindy was knowledgeable and consistently displayed a positive attitude and kind disposition. This night it was evident that she was dealing with a heavy burden in her life, and its weight was taking quite a toll.

"Cindy, are you all right?" I asked as she briskly walked toward me.

"No!" she muttered with distress in her voice.

Wondering if I could be of any assistance, I asked, "Do you want to talk about it?"

"No, I can't!" she fired back.

I got the definite feeling that whatever the problem, the subject was taboo, and I best leave it alone. Respecting her choice not to discuss her situation, I offered one more source of help. "Cindy, can I pray for you?"

She stopped, turned sharply on her heels, looked me square in the eyes, and with a softer tone of voice she said, "Donna, *that* you can do."

After that encounter, I was off work for several days, but I kept my word to Cindy. I prayed at home and in my car whenever she would pop into my mind, I would lift her up to the Lord: "Lord Jesus, I have no idea what is going on in Cindy's life, and I don't have to know. You know. You also know what she needs. Please give her the strength to get through whatever this burden is. Please help her Lord. Be very near to her Lord and provide her with the strength that she needs. She looks so tired and troubled. Please let her find her rest in You. In Jesus precious name I pray, amen."

About two weeks passed. I got off the elevators near the ER one evening and down the hall came a very familiar sight. Cindy was rushing a patient on an ER cart to the x-ray department. She spotted me and said, "Donna, don't you move! I'll be right back. You stay right here."

I waited in the hallway for Cindy to return. She came flying around the corner, stopped a few feet in front of me, and began firing questions at me in rapid succession.

"Do you remember about two weeks ago when you talked with me in ER? Did you do what you said you'd do?"

My answers were yes, and I nodded my head when she finally asked me a very pointed question "Do you believe God hears you when you pray?"

Without waiting for my response, she answered her own question. "Well, He does. You see, I had the strength to do something I didn't think that I could do. I kept asking myself, 'Where is all this strength coming from?' Then I remembered you."

Today I still have no idea what tough times this precious nurse faced.

She never asked me what I prayed for in her behalf because she already knew. I whispered her name into the amazing ear of an amazing God, and He took this woman's situation to heart. He heard my cry for help; He intervened, and when Cindy questioned the source of her strength, He pulled back the curtain of memory and reminded her that someone promised to pray.

Whenever you observe distress in another's life, you can always offer to pray. If you promise to pray for someone, please do it quickly and often. Remember that details are not important, for God knows them all. Realize that you may not always know the results of your prayers, however they have great potential to prevent, protect, and provide. Let me ask you Cindy's question: "Do you believe God hears *you* when *you* pray?" Be a believer, and know without a doubt in your heart He does!

On Call

There are several jobs in healthcare that require the responsibility of being "on-call." Working in surgery, the recovery room, or the cath lab, are just a few of the areas that utilize on-call protocol. When the day and evening shifts have completed their scheduled surgeries and procedures, the persons with call duty dons a pager or phone to respond if needed. The "on-call" staff covers any emergencies throughout the night and early morning hours or the entire weekend. In order to maintain a job with mandatory on-call requirements, individuals must be able to arrive at the hospital within a specific timeframe. When a nurse is on-call the department must be able to contact him or her whenever the need arises. The nurse must be available and respond appropriately. Have you ever considered the thought, that as Christians, we too are required to be on-call for one another?

I was working twelve-hour night shifts at Duke University Medical Center in intensive care. On my days off, I would stay up during the day and sleep at night, just like normal people! One night something woke me. I felt an urgent need to pray for a cousin I had not had any contact with for many years. I slipped out of bed and got down on my knees and prayed. Days passed and the feeling or *the call* to pray for this dear one haunted me. My prayers continued, and I enlisted Christians from my workplace and my church. Prayers were sent to heaven from North Carolina from many sincere believers. I had no details, no idea what state my relative was living in, and no understanding why the urgency— yet, we prayed. I called my grandmother time and time again. I would question her over and over "Grandma, do you know where my cousin is?"

She would always act distant and aloof and reply, "No, I have no idea."

I would plead, "Nan, she's your brother's daughter. Can't you find out?"

Nan would always seem disinterested and never pursued my request—until about one year later. I had gone to Grandma's for a vacation. As always she made all my favorite foods. We had put a ham loaf and scalloped potatoes in the oven. The coleslaw was made, and the succotash was in the heavy saucepan on the stove waiting to be warmed. Fresh yeast rolls were on the counter beside the beautiful lemon meringue pie. We had about thirty minutes before Grandpa came home from working at the State Park, so we kept to our routine. Nan and I went to her bedroom to lie down and take a quick nap. Little did I know, that this afternoon naptime was not meant for sleep; it was meant to be a rest for the soul, not the body.

"Donna," Nan began in a serious voice, "you know that I have never broken my word to your grandfather in the fifty years that I have been married to him. But for some reason I feel that I have to now. I don't understand it, but I believe that there is something you should know. Do you remember last year when you kept asking me about your cousin?"

"Yes, I remember." I knew that whatever Nan was going to divulge to me was a serious situation if Granddad had evoked a promise of secrecy.

"Well", Nan continued, "your cousin was brutally attacked and beaten. She was hospitalized for quite a while and she nearly died."

I was "on-call" that night so long ago. The Lord woke me up in the middle of the night, and I didn't hesitate. I got straight to work. I grabbed up several of my skilled co-workers and we kept at the task diligently. Did we do our job? Could it be possible that our prayers helped to save this woman's life? God alone knows that answer. He also poses all the questions, including this one, "Are you 'on-call' for God?"

The Stat Line

"Code Blue, Code Blue, Unit 1400," the voice of the hospital operator clearly rang throughout the rooms and halls of the hospital. Quickly I departed room 1012, thankful that I had completed the patient's IV and could quickly exit without explanation. As I ran to the elevator, my heart was pounding as my mind began to wonder who may be in trouble. 1400 was on the fourth floor, and I had been there just twenty minutes earlier. The elevator doors opened and I jumped in, when suddenly an ER doctor and respiratory therapist piled in beside me. They were winded and anxious to get to the patient's bedside. Adrenalin was pumping. We arrived on the fourth floor—Cardiac Care. The elevator doors opened to reveal the sight of caregivers responding to the code in room 1409 bed 2. The staff had removed Mr. Jones from bed 1 to a wheelchair in the lobby. It was a Sunday afternoon, and the hallway was lined with visitors and curious bystanders. As we entered 1409, we each knew our purpose and job. Automatic pilot took over, and the scene looked like this:

The RN at the crash cart grabbed the EKG pads and quickly placed them appropriately on Mr. T's chest.

The respiratory therapist was at the head of the bed in the process of intubating the patient, maintaining the airway, and delivering lifesaving oxygen.

An RN was on Mr. T's chest performing chest compression.

I placed a tourniquet on Mr. T's arm to obtain an IV line so that medications and fluids could be delivered into his circulatory system.

The RN in charge of Mr. T's care automatically began to expound on the medical history and precipitating events of Mr. T's cardiac episode.

The physicians discussed the heart rhythm and called out orders accordingly.

The nursing supervisor was feverishly documenting the many simultaneous events as they occurred.

The chaplain was comforting the family.

Call a Code Blue in a hospital and you will receive a stat response. STAT—immediately drop what you are doing and get here now. Someone's life may depend upon your response.

Have you lived through a time of crisis? Have you had to call for help? Did anyone come when you called? Did someone skilled arrive on the scene, look at you with a dumb stare and do nothing? Have you ever dialed 911? Can you imagine dialing 911 and getting a busy signal—or an answering machine?

If humans are able to set up an emergency system to help other humans through physical crises, do you believe that God could provide a means for us to reach Him in times of critical need as well?

Imagine for just a moment, God, in His infinite Glory in the throne room of heaven, surrounded by His angels. A messenger appears (probably Gabriel), with a red telephone. He approaches the Almighty and bowing his knees in reverence he announces, "Your Grace, the STAT line has been ringing all morning." Suppose for a moment that you are the one making the call. In your mind, how do you see God responding to you?

Perhaps you are someone who never calls Him in the first place so you could care less if He answers the phone. You wouldn't know what to say.

You call God, now and then, but you know that He is busy and you only call when you really feel it's necessary. If He doesn't answer you, well, you understand that it's got to be difficult running the universe. Maybe He will get back to you later.

Yes, you called, but perhaps your timing was off. His timing is perfect. He will answer you, *In His Time*. Could there be anyone bold and brazen enough to believe that a stat call will be answered, and a response will be immediate? Stat prayer; stat response.

We can all believe that God does do things according to His heavenly timetable. However, I believe that sometimes His timetable includes a STAT response to a person's STAT prayer. Immediate divine intervention is something that we can believe is possible.

How often in the Bible do people receive stat answers to their prayers? Consider one of my favorite passages found in 2 Kings 20: 1-6 (*italics* mine):

In those days Hezekiah became ill and was at the point of death. The prophet Isaiah son of Amoz went to him and said,

"This is what the Lord says: Put your house in order, because you are going to die: you will not recover." Hezekiah turned his face to the wall and prayed to the Lord, "Remember, O Lord, how I have walked before you faithfully and with wholehearted devotion and have done what is good in your eyes." And Hezekiah wept bitterly. *Before Isaiah had left the middle court, the word of the Lord came to him:* "Go back and tell Hezekiah, the leader of my people, 'This is what the Lord, the God of your father David, says: I have heard your prayer and seen your tears; *I will heal you.* On the third day from now you will go up to the temple of the Lord. I will add fifteen years to your life. And I will deliver you and this city from the hand of the king of Assyria. I will defend this city for my sake and for the sake of my servant David." Hezekiah cried out to God. God heard his cry and also saw the tears streaming down his face. God stopped Isaiah in his tracks and had him return to Hezekiah with the new message. "You have fifteen more years of life."

Another documentation of such a rapid request and response occurs in Luke 8: 41-48. This story is often identified as the miracle on the way to a miracle. Jesus was on his way to the home of Jarius to tend to his dying twelve-year-old daughter. The crowds were pressing in on Christ and His disciples.

Now when Jesus returned, a crowd welcomed him, for they were all expecting him. Then a man named Jairus, a ruler of the synagogue, came and fell at Jesus' feet, pleading with him to come to his house because his only daughter, a girl of about twelve, was dying.
As Jesus was on his way, the crowds almost crushed him. And a woman was there who had been subject to bleeding for twelve years, but no one could heal her. She came up behind him and touched the edge of his cloak, and immediately her bleeding stopped.
"Who touched me?" Jesus asked. When they all denied it, Peter said, "Master, the people are crowding and pressing against you."

But Jesus said, "Someone touched me; I know that power has gone out from me."

Then the woman, seeing that she could not go unnoticed, came trembling and fell at his feet. In the presence of all the people, she told why she had touched him and how she had been instantly healed. Then he said to her, "Daughter, your faith has healed you. Go in peace."

I have often wondered if Luke the physician knew of this woman and the multiple treatments that were unsuccessful. She believed and through her act of faith, she received a stat response in her situation.

Remember the leper that Christ healed in Mark 1:40-42?

A man with leprosy came to him and begged him on his knees, "If you are willing, you can make me clean." Filled with compassion, Jesus reached out his hand and touched the man, "I am willing," he said. "Be clean."

Immediately, the leprosy left him and he was cured.

These three examples are not the only ones that illustrate a very rapid response from God when His people were in great need. In the Old Testament, as well as the New, there are many stories that reveal God responding to a crisis. Parting the Red Sea is another marvelous example. But does God intervene in our lives today with rapid responses? Consider the following stories and draw your own conclusions!

Prune Power?

I was on a team for a Christian retreat, and the lay director introduced me to a lovely young woman who was having a personal problem of a physical nature. Usually at a retreat the focus is on Christ and not on individual accomplishments or what one does for a living. However, I was introduced as a nurse in hopes that I could provide this woman with some suggestions.

Ms. V. confided in me that she suffers from Crohn's disease that had been under control for quite some time. She began her story, "I am so very disappointed. I was so excited to be here and I just want to absorb every word that the Lord has for me. But I can't! I'm constipated and miserable, there is swelling down there and I can't even sit comfortably. I guess I'll just have to spend the rest of the weekend standing in back of the conference room."

Break time was over and everyone returned to the conference room except for Janie—one of the pastors—and me. She was grazing on the munchies at the snack table when I quickly approached her with my request. "Pastor Janie, we need to pray now. Would you please pray with me? We have a young woman who is having troubles."

Pastor Janie did not refuse me, so we held hands and bowed our heads and hearts right there at the snack table. I began, "Lord Jesus, Ms. V. is having troubles. She is constipated, swollen, and miserable. She came here seeking Your every word. She is terribly disappointed and needs Your intervention. Lord, help her now please. Take care of her constipation and make the swelling go away stat, Lord. Because we know You are able and merciful. In Jesus' name. This is my prayer."

Then the pastor began, "Now Lord, it isn't as if we are telling you what to do... if it be your will... in Your time... in Jesus name, Amen."

I just couldn't hold back, so I added, "But Lord, *now* would be so nice."

In just a few minutes Ms. V. came around the corner and she said, "I think I may have to make a trip to the lady's room."

The lay director, abreast of the situation, then came to me with a mission of mercy. "Donna, go to my room. I have soft toilet paper on the shelf behind the door. Please take it to Ms. V." So, I retrieved the stash of soft toilet paper and headed to the campground bathroom. "Oh Ms. V.," I announced, "The lay director sent me to give you some soft toilet paper."

Suddenly the stall door opened and Ms. V. walked out and replied, "I don't need it now. I've already gone to the bathroom, and I know this sounds funny, but I do believe the swelling has gone down."

I smiled a bit sheepishly and said, "I need to confess something to you. As soon as you told me your problem, I grabbed one of the pastors and we prayed for you."

She smiled and said, "Thank you so much!" and she made her way back to the conference room, while I returned to my duties as weekend helper. One of the team members aware of Ms. V.'s circumstances asked me how she was doing. I smiled and told her, "all systems go." The team member's response was "must have been the prunes."

The next day Ms V. gave me the biggest hug and sincerely thanked me again. I told her that some on the team were giving glory to the prunes. Ms. V.'s response to such a thought was, "Oh, NO! Prunes don't have that kind of *power*!"

Hey Baby, It's Cold Outside

J.W. woke up early the morning of December 23, to witness one of the heaviest blankets of snow the Midwest had encountered in years. His wife made the decision to stay home from work, but J.W. felt he had an obligation to the patients and visitors who would be coming to the outpatient surgery center. The drive to work was uneventful, and J.W. began to clear walkways and shovel the sidewalks as soon as he arrived. It was difficult to keep things clear for the snowfall was relentless. Patients began to call and cancel as soon as the center was open. Thus the center made the decision to close and send the staff home.

When J.W. drove to work there was an accumulation of six to eight inches on the ground, but now that amount had doubled. The drive home would not be as easy as the drive to work had been. In his mind, J.W. began to consider the best way to get home. He wanted to avoid curves and hills if at all possible. He had traveled Oak Grove Road on the way to work and had no trouble, so he decided to return home by the same route.

J.W. tells his story:

As I approached Oak Grove Road there stood a deputy sheriff rerouting traffic. They had closed the road. I turned around and got onto the expressway, which was moving very slowly. The road was not cleared very well. Some places it was one lane and in others it was two lanes, so I got off and decided to try Epworth Road and then I could get onto Oak Grove from the back way. I admit that I was nervous, and I kept praying to God to please get me home safely.

The snow was blowing so very hard that the windshield wipers were icing up. I could see that no one was behind me so I stopped and cleaned the wipers off. I turned onto Oak Grove and within minutes I hit the ice.

My truck slid off the side of the road, missing the twelve-foot deep ditch by less than a foot. My heart was pounding so hard, I felt it was going to beat right out of my chest. I cried out, "God! What am I going to do now?" I had not noticed before but there were taillights from other cars off the road ahead of me. I was scared, pretty bad. I tried to rock the truck back and forth a little to try to get back on the road. My efforts were futile.

I wished that I had heeded the warning that they had closed this road for a reason, but I didn't. A four-wheel-drive truck drove by me. They went down the road past me a ways and could not get through. I watched as he turned around and came back toward me. I hoped he would stop, maybe pull me out or at least call for help for me. He did stop and offered his cell phone, but my fingers and hands were so cold and shaky, I wasn't able to dial. They offered me a ride back toward the highway and I took it. We talked about the severity of the weather and then we parted ways.

These kind people dropped me off about a mile and a half from my home. I began the long walk home. I didn't really begin to feel the effects of the cold, wind and snow, until I crossed the highway. Trudging through that blizzard on foot, I became colder than I have ever been in my life. The cold became more intense with every step I took. I walked by a van that was just parked by the road and I remember thinking that it must have been stuck in the snow just like my truck. I had left my gloves in the truck without thinking and my hands were freezing.

Each step was more difficult than the one before and I remember thinking, *I'm dying*. I could not breathe and my heart felt like it was about to explode in my chest. I kept saying to myself, *I'm not going to make it*. In desperation I finally cried out, "God, I need some help here!" I continued to walk and I thought if I could just make it up to one of the houses up the road I would be okay. Yet, they seemed so far away. I actually felt myself slipping away.

Suddenly, that van I had seen earlier pulled up beside me, and the people said, "Get in." Without hesitation, I got in. They asked me how far I was going. I had a hard time telling them, but I somehow managed to give them directions. They talked to me, but I have no recollection of that conversation. They drove me all the way home.

J.W. cried out to God in the midst of a storm, and God not only heard his cry, but responded immediately in his time of crisis by providing a van with compassionate people that safely carried him home.

J.W. continued to reflect about that day:

We never know what the day will bring, but He does. God heard every one of my prayers that day, from the time I got up that morning until I walked back into my house physically and emotionally exhausted. Prayer is a powerful tool that gives us fellowship and access to our Savior. When we cry out to Him, He hears and He responds. Why does He? Only, because He, as our Heavenly Father, protects and loves each one of His children.

Whenever I think back on that day when it was so cold outside and I felt like my life was slipping away, my heart fills with thankfulness, for God was merciful and chose to spare my life. God saved me spiritually, the day that He sent His Son to die for my sins. Now, I know He saved me physically as well. He is my God and I am His child.

So my lesson is, "Hey Baby, when it's cold outside, pray to the one who saves the body and the soul. Never forget He is your Father and He consistently protects and watches over His own."

It is comforting and exciting to review times when our prayers are answered swiftly and creatively by our God. Does He love us any less when we don't receive the answer that we long for? Is He preoccupied or ignoring us when we plead with Him and our heart's desire never is fulfilled? Many of us are familiar with the difficulty of understanding why some sincere and persistent prayers are placed before our Father and His response isn't quick or comforting. How can we explain God's choice to delay? How does a person continue to believe when the miracle does not come? Perhaps we all can gain some insight from a young boy named Colin. Open your ears and your hearts to the message he has prepared for us. Colin is preaching a hard lesson that is meant to offer us a measure of comfort and healing we so desperately need.

"Mommy, Why Won't God Heal Brubbie?"

The precious eleven-year-old lies in a hospital bed in ICU for the last time, his little body imprisoned by a deep coma. When he was six years old, he had developed viral encephalitis, and its complications robbed him of his speech, mobility, and childhood. The only thing this sweet boy ever wanted to be when he grew up was a preacher. Both his grandparents and parents followed the Lord with the deepest devotion.

One night Colin's little sister approached her mother with a heart full of confusion and sadness. She asked a very grown-up question, "Mommy, I pray for Brubbie every night. Why doesn't God make him well?"

I can only imagine how often any mother asks God that same question when a child so loved is in an incapacitated state. As Christians, we hold to Scripture as our guide—our how-to-book, our complete spiritual reference—the book which contains all the answers.

In Matthew 17:20, the disciples were unable to cast out a devil from a little boy. When they asked Christ why their attempts failed, Jesus replied, "Because you have so little faith. I tell you the truth, if you have faith as small as a mustard seed; you can say to this mountain move from here to there and it will move. Nothing will be impossible for you."

How about the scripture in John 14:13-14, "And I will do whatever you ask in my name, so that the Son may bring glory to the Father. You can ask me for anything in my name and I will do it."

I can promise you that this family and many Christian families know these scriptures by heart and often cry out to God "in Jesus name" and their children do not receive miraculous healing. I would also imagine that they would begin to doubt their faith and perhaps carry guilt and shame in their hearts believing that due to some sin or lack of faith they were to blame for their son's plight. They are often haunted with this devastating thought that they simply do not have enough faith to "pray their child back to a state of health".

One of the greatest privileges I have ever had in my Christian life has been crossing paths with Colin's dear family. Gathered around this child one afternoon in their living room, I had an opportunity to pray for him. I will never forget the handful of dear people including his tiny sisters in a circle around this young boy in their living room. As we sat on the floor holding hands, we all prayed earnestly. Yet, it was his father's broken-hearted cry that to this day brings me to tears. Tears were flowing down this dear father's face as he honestly cried out, "I miss him so much." That day I became aware of an undeniable truth. The pain within the heart of loving parents is so untouched by time. The longing for health and wholeness for their child is a daily anguish and desire that burns deep within their hearts. So why wouldn't God heal Brubbie? Why didn't a miracle happen? God would have received all the glory and honor.

Complete physical healing for Colin did not take place, however there were definite times of miracles along this family's journey. The Lord was with them through it all. The hardest time for Colin's mother was when he suffered seizures. It was nearly more than she could bear. She found herself asking God how suffering seizures *nonstop* could possibly be His will. They were at a hospital in Indianapolis where they had spent multiple visits throughout the years. They had established a precious church family in Indy and had made several valuable relationships. The physicians were running out of potential therapy options to curtail the seizure activity and suggested that Colin be transferred to the Children's Hospital in Cincinnati, Ohio. So Colin and his family made the trip.

One day while at the hospital, two men approached Colin's mom and dad. They introduced themselves as friends of the pastor's son from the Indianapolis church, and they had come to pray for Colin. Always happy for any prayer, the family introduced these men to Colin, they prayed and went on their way. The next day Colin's mom looked up and walking down the hall toward her were the same two men who had come the day before. They explained their presence.

"Tammy, we hope that you don't mind, but we felt we should come back and pray for Colin once again. You see, both of us dreamt of your son all night last night, and we believe that God wants us to pray for him again today."

And these men prayed for Colin. Colin had three seizures that day. Then he was seizure-free for an entire year.

The prophet Joel provides evidence of the Holy Spirit in regards to future events and he states in chapter 2:28 "I will pour out my spirit on all people. Your sons and daughters will prophesy, your old men will dream dreams, your young men will see visions."

Is it possible for God to meet us in our dreams even today? If we believe that God's word crosses all time barriers, this question is answered without any doubt by the following scriptures:

Is anything too hard for the Lord? (Gen. 18:14)

For nothing is impossible with God (Luke 1:37).

Brubbie wanted to be a minister like his grandfather. His life of inability revealed a message more potent than any sermon delivered from a pulpit. He was totally dependent on his family for every aspect of his life. God placed infirmity upon a child so that anyone who knew this child's family could see what Jesus looks like!

The funeral home was packed as long lines wound around to the outside door. This one little life touched so many people. The enduring love and continuous task of caring for their son at home day after day was an expression of Godliness. He was growing so tall and heavy that his mother had developed a bad back, yet he never missed his rehab or physical therapy appointments. Her life song would include these lyrics, "He's not heavy, he's my son."

Colin's liver malfunctioned at the end and his blood clotting mechanisms failed. Faith. Did Colin's mother lack faith? In the five and one half years that she cared for her son, there may have been times when her faith wavered or even fell flat. Yet her faith amazed me. While her little boy suffered a bleed into his head, pushing dangerously on vital centers in his brain, her comment to me was, "Donna, God could heal him even tonight and that would be okay with me". Faith. This woman had such faith. They never doubted God could miraculously heal their son. God gave Colin heavenly healing. His family grieves his death. They all "miss him so much," yet they rejoice in the fact that he is free at last in a heavenly body to talk and run and play. Anyone who wonders why God would not heal little Colin may consider the story of the Roman centurion.

When Jesus had entered Capernaum, a centurion came to him, asking for help.

"Lord," he said, "my servant lies at home paralyzed and in terrible suffering." Jesus said to him, "I will go and heal him." The centurion replied, "Lord, I do not deserve to have you come under my roof. But just say the word, and my servant will be healed. For I myself am a man under authority, with soldiers under me. I tell this one, 'Go", and he goes; and that one, 'Come,' and he comes. I say to my servant, 'Do this,' and he does it."

When Jesus heard this, he was astonished and said to those following him, "I tell you the truth, I have not found anyone in Israel with such great faith" (Matt. 8:5-10).

Then Jesus said to the centurion, "Go! It will be done just as you believed it would." And his servant was healed at that very hour (8:13).

Just as Christ stood in awe of the faith of this Roman, many who know Colin's family stand in awe for they held to their faith *even when they did not receive the healing.* This family loved this boy unconditionally and showed those of us who knew of their situation exactly what faith and works is all about. Their church family reached out in love and support, and the body of Christ was united in prayer and action. This dear family was never alone. Galatians 6:2 states, "Carry each other's burdens, and in this way you will fulfill the law of Christ."

Colin did preach with his short life. His sermon embraced the topics of dependence and commitment. Daily his family cared for his every need. Daily God will care for your every need, if only you relinquish your independence and become totally reliant upon your Heavenly Father. In the event that you have fallen away from your God, Colin wants you to know that you are breaking His heart. *God misses you so much.* Let Him love you and carry you. No matter what your situation, *never* let go of your faith!

If you are a caregiver and you are weighted down with your responsibilities, here are a few of the scriptures that helped Colin's mother to get through tough times. Her prayer for you is that you hold to your faith and gain strength and comfort from her experience. Cling to these precious passages from God. Gain a Godly understanding of suffering and perseverance. Continue to care and never forget that your acts of love are never in vain. On the tough days, reread the passage from Matthew and remember the one who you are truly caring for and serving. May God bless you mightily as you continue to give your all for that precious someone in your life!

Therefore, since we have been justified through faith, we have peace with God through our Lord Jesus Christ, through whom we have gained access by faith into this grace in which we now stand. And we rejoice in the hope of the glory of God. Not only so, but we also rejoice in our sufferings, because we know that suffering produces perseverance; perseverance, character; and character, hope. And hope does not disappoint us, because God has poured out his love into our hearts by the Holy Spirit, whom he has given us (Rom. 5:1-5).

I consider that our present sufferings are not worth comparing with the glory that will be revealed in us (Rom. 8:18).

Consider it pure joy, my brothers, whenever you face trials of many kinds, because you know that the testing of your faith develops perseverance. Perseverance must finish its work so that you may be mature and complete, not lacking anything (James 1:2-4).

Let us hold unswervingly to the hope we profess, for he who promised is faithful. And let us consider how we may spur one another on toward love and good deeds (Heb. 10:23-24).

"When the Son of Man comes in his glory, and all the angels with him, he will sit on his throne in heavenly glory. All the nations will be gathered before him, and he will separate the people one from another as a shepherd separates the sheep from the goats. He will put the sheep on his right and the goats on his left. Then the King will say to those on his right, 'Come you who are blessed by my Father; take your inheritance, the kingdom prepared for you since the creation of the world. For I was hungry and you gave me something to eat, I was thirsty and you gave me something to drink, I was a stranger and you invited me in, I needed clothes and you clothed me, I was sick and you looked after me, I was in prison and you came to visit me.' Then the righteous will answer him, 'Lord, when did we see you hungry and feed you, or thirsty and give you something to drink? When did we see you a stranger and invite you in, or needing clothes and clothe you? When did we see you sick or in prison and go to visit you?' Then the King will reply, '*I tell you the truth, whatever you did for one of the least of these, brothers of mine, you did it for Me!*'" (Matt. 25:1-14, *italics* added).

5. Expectations and Promises

THERE IS ONE THING THAT is impossible for God to do: God cannot lie. Repeatedly in the Old and New Testaments there are countless situations where the Lord has proved Himself over and over again. Have you ever noticed that often when God makes a promise to us He loves to use the phrase "*I will?*" Whenever He says, "*I will*," He is saying:

"I choose to, with certainty."

"I have made a firm choice."

"I am resolved and determined to."

"Count on this with complete probability and total expectation."

When God speaks the words "*I will*," we cannot doubt, nor can we ignore the magnitude of His statements included in these scriptures. These are concrete, absolute promises from God that need examination and application in our lives.

> "For if you forgive men when they sin against you, your Heavenly Father *will* also forgive you" (Matt. 6:14, *italics* added).

> "Whoever acknowledges me before men *I will* acknowledge him before my Father in heaven" (Matt. 10:32, *italics* added).

"For the Son of Man is going to come in His Father's glory with His angels and then *he will* reward each person according to what he has done" (Matt. 16:27, *italics* added).

Can you see the pattern? Can you also see that His promises to us are connected to or dependent upon our actions? May I suggest that *our life choices activate His promises.*

Imagine that you have decided to make grilled chicken tonight for supper, and you marinated the raw poultry and placed it in a container in the refrigerator. You cleaned and prepared the grill, filled it with charcoal, carefully sprayed the coals with lighter fluid, and then realized that you were out of matches. You had no means to start the fire. No catalyst to ignite a flame. No source of heat to change your raw, flavor-filled chicken into the primary portion of a delectable edible meal.

So it is with the promises of God. Our preparation and our choices must be thorough, deliberate, and complete. Our actions provide the catalyst for God to ignite His fire in our lives and release His innumerable promises, therefore grilling them into our hearts so that we can have fully cooked faith! So many people want to cling to His promises without any acknowledgement that God expects us to be active participants, not just idle recipients.

So what must we do to choose wisely? What can we possibly use as our measuring apparatus to determine if our decisions are level and straight? I believe we must begin with the One who holds in His hand the only standard stick or ruler that matters. We need to observe each area that our Lord has included for assessment. I believe that we must be weighed and measured. The greatest hope for us all is accepting the fact that God has been extremely clear about His proposals and His purposes for those who call themselves *Christians*. We have His Word and a variety of stories that identify ways to initiate His positive and negative actions. I am convinced that through the identification and sincere allegiance to *His expectations*, each one of us can become a conduit where His Holy Spirit and all His attributes may freely flow through our hearts, our hands, and our minds. His promises are steadfast and sure. However, we must live our lives with an unquenchable desire to meet His expectations.

Let us consider this question: What does God expect from us? I believe the Bible is stuffed full of answers. He has told us through His relationships with others exactly what He expects. In my examination of this question I have found the following to be some of the expectations that are of utmost importance to God: honor, giving, forgiving, and love saturated with obedience. A review of His Word reveals the depth of pain and disgust His people are capable of producing within the heart of God whenever these areas are neglected or ignored. When we evaluate the expectations of God, it is only His perspective that we need. Let us begin to research honor by listening attentively to the prophets Daniel and Malachi.

God Expects Honor

Daniel 5:1-30 is the complete text for this review. King Belshazzar was feasting with his nobles. They were drinking wine when the king made an extremely poor decision. He gave instructions to his servants to bring out the gold and silver goblets that King Nebuchadnezzar had stolen from the temple in Jerusalem. The purpose of his request was not just to "show off" his goods, but to drink their wine from these sacred treasures. Their transgression against God did not stop with this action. They slapped God in the face with blatant disrespect as they began to praise the gods of gold, silver, bronze, iron, wood, and stone.

"Suddenly the fingers of a human hand appeared and wrote on the plaster of the wall, near the lamp stand in the royal palace. The king watched the hand as it wrote. His face turned pale and he was so frightened that his knees knocked together and his legs gave way" (Dan. 5:5-6).

So the story continues, and the king proceeds to call all of the mystics and the astrologers to read the writing on the wall. No one was able to achieve this task. Then the queen stepped in and informed the king that there is a man in the kingdom with the ability to interpret dreams, explain riddles, and solve difficult problems. The queen explains that during the reign of King Nebechadnezzer, this man had been appointed chief of the magicians, enchanters, astrologers, and diviners due to his insight, intelligence, and wisdom. Thus Daniel was summoned and the king offered him gifts and position in return for his reading the writing on the wall. Daniel proceeded to expound to the king:

"O king, the Most High God gave your father Nebuchadnezzar sovereignty and greatness and glory and splendor. Because of the high position he gave him, all the peoples and nations and men of every language dreaded and feared him. Those the king wanted to put to death, he put to death; those he wanted to spare, he spared; those he wanted to promote, he promoted; and those he wanted to humble, he humbled. But when *his heart became arrogant and hardened with pride*, he was deposed from his royal throne and stripped of his glory. He was driven away from people and given the mind of an animal; he lived with the wild donkeys and ate grass like cattle; and his body was drenched with the dew of heaven, *until he acknowledged that the Most High God is sovereign over the kingdoms of men* and sets over them anyone he wishes. But you his son, O Belshazzar, have not humbled yourself though you knew all this. Instead, you have set yourself up against the Lord of heaven. You had the goblets from his temple brought to you, and you and your nobles, your wives and your concubines drank wine from them. *You praised the gods of silver and gold, of bronze, iron, wood and stone, which cannot see or hear or understand. But you did not honor the God who holds in His hand your life and all your ways.* Therefore he sent the hand that wrote the inscription. This is the inscription that was written: Mene, Mene, Tekel, Parsin. This is what these words mean:

"Mene: God has numbered the days of your reign and brought it to an end.

"Tekel: You have been weighed on the scales and found wanting.

"Parsin: Your kingdom is divided and given to the Medes and Persians."

Then at Belshazzar's command, Daniel was clothed in purple, a gold chain was placed around his neck, and he was proclaimed the third highest ruler in the kingdom. That very night Belshazzar, king of the Babylonians was slain, and Darius the Mede took over the kingdom at the age of sixty-two (Daniel 5:18-30, *italics* added).

This story provides so many important elements for us to internalize. We must guard our hearts from arrogance and pride and be aware that false gods can steal away our position in the family of God. Honoring God requires our total acknowledgement of who He is. Matthew 10:32 shows us the positive benefit of acknowledging God before men. In turn, He will acknowledge us before God, the Heavenly Father. Read further for verse 33 plainly provides us with another promise: "But whoever disowns me before men, I will disown him before my Father in heaven."

Do you honor the God who holds in His hand your life and all your ways?

The concept of honoring God is vitally important for us to understand. In the book of Malachi, this issue is clearly addressed. God's words are packed full of emotion, and we can actually feel His outrage and pain when those He loves choose not to love or honor Him.

The Book of Malachi is only four chapters long, yet this tiny book provides us with *really big* principles. The priests and the people were offending God. God let them know that He was very much aware of their contemptible practices and blatant disobedience! God begins His rebuke by making this statement in chapter 1 verse 2, "I have loved you," says the Lord.

Then God poses this question: "Where is the honor and respect that I deserve?" The Lord was upset that the priests were not sacrificing the pure, spotless, unblemished animals. Instead they were bringing diseased and crippled ones for sacrifice. That practice was a deliberate insult and screamed of total disrespect for the expectations of God. Bringing a pure animal gave meaning to the word sacrifice. Bringing a crippled animal reduced the term of offering to merely a burning of the undesirable. The choices made by the priests were intolerable to God because *true sacrifice costs*!

"Cursed is the cheat who has an acceptable male in his flock and vows to give it, but then sacrifices a blemished animal to the Lord. For I am a great King, says the Lord Almighty and my name is to be feared among the nations" (Mal. 1:14).

God then explains how to remedy this situation. He never reveals a problem without providing the appropriate solution. He informs the priest of the appropriate actions they must take. God firmly states His expectation and connects it with a promise that is not pleasant!

"*If* you do not listen, and *if* you do not set your heart to honor my name' says the Lord Almighty, 'I will send a curse upon you and I will curse your blessings. Yes, I have already cursed them, because *you have not set your heart to honor me*'" (Ma. 2:2, *italics* added). God expects honor from His people. *The World Book Dictionary* defines honor as a verb meaning: to adore, to worship, to show respect to, to highly regard, to think highly of.

When we read Malachi today, we realize that our relationship with the Lord is so changed. We no longer live under the Old Testament law that required a sacrifice to cover our sins. Regardless of this change in practice, no one is exempt from honoring God with our lives today. Just as God began His rebuke of the priests, He could easily say to each of us, "*I have loved you.*" I believe His rebuke has the potential to be so much more severe. God has every right to inquire of us what we have done with His sacrifice. John 3:16-17 states that God gave His Son. God sent His Son. So in obedience to God, Christ came from heaven not only to perform the acceptable duties of the holy priesthood but also to be the absolute, perfect, sacrificial lamb. His obedience and willingness to be slaughtered was an act of pure and sacred love. It is the love of Christ at Calvary that showed the world the one and only lasting sacrifice acceptable to our Holy God. God accepted His son's blood offering, took away all of our sins, dipped believers in forgiveness and coated us with the righteousness of Christ. Only through this God-directed process can anyone give pleasure and honor to the Lord God Almighty.

God provided the sacrificial lamb. How are you handling the most costly sacrifice the world has ever known? Jesus Christ is perfect in every way. We need to acknowledge that God provided His son for us. Give Him respect and honor. He deserves it. Consider the following scriptures:

In the story of Moses and the burning bush, God explains to Moses His plan to rescue His people from the oppression of Pharaoh and the

Egyptians. Moses asks God this question: "Suppose I go to the Israelites and say to them, 'The god of your fathers has sent me to you,' and they ask me, 'What is his name?' Then what shall I tell them?" God said to Moses, "I AM WHO I AM. This is what you are to say to the Israelites: 'I AM' has sent you" (Exodus 3:1-14).

God is the great I AM. Do we truly see Him as He is? Let us look through the eyes of the prophet Isaiah to get a permanent picture in our minds of the majesty and glory of our God.

"In the year that King Uzziah died, I saw the Lord seated on a throne, high and exalted, and the train of his robe filled the temple. Above him were seraphs, each with six wings: with two wings they covered their faces, with two they covered their feet, and with two they were flying. And they were calling to one another: 'Holy, Holy, Holy is the Lord Almighty; the whole earth is full of His glory'" (Isa. 6:1-3).

In the book of Job, chapters 38 –41 tell the magnificent knowledge and infinite greatness of God. He presents Job with many questions and mysteries. He speaks of laying the foundation of the earth, the boundaries of the sea and clouds, and the residence of light and darkness. He asks if Job is aware where the storehouses of snow and hail are kept. He describes His hand of control over lightning and thunder. He talks of His eyes watching mountain goats and deer give birth. He speaks eloquently of the animal kingdom, revealing His power over them. In Job 41:11, the Lord speaks, "Who has a claim against me that I must pay? Everything under heaven belongs to me."

We must honor and respect God for who He is and what He has done. Never forget that He has loved you. Set your heart to give Him the honor and respect that He deserves. Daily, remember He is the God who holds in His hand your life and all your ways. Contemplate His greatness and all that He has done to save your life. Pursue a life that honors God and take to heart His promises found in I Samuel 2:30: "Those who honor me I *will* honor, but those who despise me *will be* disdained" (*italics* added).

God Expects Giving

"'There will always be poor people in the land. Therefore I command you to be openhanded toward your brothers and toward the poor and needy in your land'"(Deut. 15:11).

"A generous man will himself be blessed, for he shares his food with the poor" (Prov. 22:9).

When the time of year comes for the pastor to address the dreaded subject of *tithing*, the topic is to parishioners what Deep Woods Off! bug spray is to ticks and mosquitoes. The word tithe is a repellant. The congregation would love for the minister to lay "OFF" the subject entirely, and often they don't attend church during this particular series of sermons.

God has blessed us mightily, and giving back a portion of what He has given us to support His ministry, feed someone hungry, or provide medical supplies and aid to the sick should be something Christians want to do.

We are such strange people. We love God to pour out His blessings upon us, yet we want to dam up the flow so that we can bask in the blessings ourselves. Remember *S*-elfish *I*-n *N*-ature spells *SIN*. Sharing our blessings and living a generous life should be one of our greatest joys. Generosity is a sign of Christianity as well as an action that God has provided an expectation connected to a positive promise.

"Give, and *it will* be given to you. A good measure, pressed down, shaken together and running over, *will be* poured into your lap. For with the measure you use, it *will be* measured to you" (Luke 6:38, *italics* added).

There is no greater joy in my life than giving. That is my feeling today, yet I must confess that this has been one area that I am sure I have disappointed God through neglect and selfishness. My attitude changed drastically when I began reading the prophets in my personal Bible study, for I learned that tithing is a serious area that shows our complete dependence on God. It is an act of commitment and obedience that I believe many people would prefer to neglect and ignore. When I found myself face-to-face with God's unmistakable feeling about my reluctance to give him *my* money, I had a major change of heart. He presented me with a challenge which I accepted it, and I have no regrets.

Don't Be a Robber

"Will a man rob God? Yet you rob me. But you ask, 'How do we rob you?'

"In tithes and offerings. You are under a curse, the whole nation of you because you are robbing me. Bring the whole tithe into the storehouse, that there may be food in my house."

"*Test me in this,*," says the Lord Almighty, "See if I will not throw open the floodgates of heaven and pour out so much blessing that you will not have room enough for it" (Mal. 3:8-10, *italics* added).

So my husband and I began to tithe. It was amazing to me that I always had extra money, even though I was giving my tithe. I was always in awe whenever God would orchestrate His blessings. Once I received a letter from a ministry that had blessed my life tremendously. They never asked for monies, but in this letter they stated that they had an opportunity to purchase a prime piece of land that they would use to build a Christian school. I sent them a check for $250.00. Can you imagine my surprise when I went to work that same week and found an unexpected envelope in my mailbox? The hospital gave all the nurses a special bonus check, and you can guess the amount: $250.00.

You, too, can begin to see God at work in your personal financial situation the moment that you stop robbing Him. All that we have comes from His hand, and He clearly expects us to give back to Him a portion of our blessings. Have you ever been to the ocean and enjoyed the consistent flow of waves? They never stop coming to the shore. When we give back to God, our blessings ride the waves of generosity and continuity for the work of God. We need to have an attitude adjustment when we think about tithing.

Let us begin by taking a truthful look at the church that you attend. Can you imagine God giving you responsibility to help care for His house? It requires upkeep. There are bills that need to be paid—heating, cooling, electric, and water to name just a few. You go to worship expecting to have comfortable seats, clean floors, properly controlled temperature, adequate lighting, working microphones, a great PA system and then, of course, you expect a good sermon from the preacher, and a great time in worship from the choir director and all the musicians. You have expectations.

So does God. You know what it takes to maintain your own home. God's house needs maintenance, too. Your church is God's house. Your support is required. Providing for God's ministry is your responsibility and when you neglect your responsibility, *you rob God.* Consider the magnitude of this next statement:

> When your expectations override God's expectations
> You take away His joy,
> You rob him of His pleasure because
> You steal from God an opportunity to bless the lives of others with a portion of the very blessings He has so generously bestowed upon your life.

Everything that you have, every dollar that you make, belongs to God. He does not ask you for 90 percent of your living. What if He did? What if He required 90 percent, but took 100 percent from you instead? Would you be upset? How do you think He feels when He asks you for 10 percent and gets 0 percent? You may believe that you don't have enough money in your bank account to tithe, but look closely at your check register. What you spend your time and money on are your priorities.

Do you eat out? Why not forego a meal at an expensive restaurant and eat a peanut butter and jelly sandwich? Then give the money you would have spent at the restaurant back to God.

Here is a challenge for the fashion kings and queens among us: can you go through your clothes closets and chests of drawers and convince yourselves that you will wear all those items in this lifetime? Look once more with this prayer in your heart, "Lord, what items hanging in this closet do You need to clothe someone?" I am sure you can find something to give away.

Perhaps you just can't give up *your* things. Do you keep boxes of children's clothes in your attic because they belonged to *your* babies? As your children grew, the number of boxes increased and now you have enough merchandise in storage to open your own children's clothing store. If only we could see the other little ones who would love to wear the things that we so neatly have tucked away. Would it be difficult for you to give away these outfits that are so dear to your heart? Yes, it definitely would be hard. However, that very difficulty is pleasing to God for it would be a sacrifice. Give them up and let God give you something that money cannot buy: *the joy of being an anonymous giver.*

Do you have a craft? Do you work with wood? Do you sew, knit, or crochet? One day, I called the Methodist Youth Home wanting to do something special. I asked if there was anything that they needed. I told them that I could sew. They were thrilled that I had offered. The cooks in the kitchen needed aprons. I had a blast making aprons for people I have never met who work in a kitchen and feed and serve young teen mothers and their babies. There are always ways to give back to God. If He has given you a gift, be creative and find a way to use it.

In 2 Corinthians 9:6-15 is a marvelous passage on generosity. Verse 7 states, "Each man should give what he has decided in his heart to give, not reluctantly or under compulsion, for God loves a cheerful giver."

Whenever the subject of tithing is preached and anytime the offering plate is passed, remember that paper money and coins represent blessings from God to you. So whenever you pull a portion out of your purse, wallet, or pocket, do it with the same attitude of joy that the Lord experienced when He first gave you the blessing.

In Matthew 10, Christ gave instructions to His disciples as He sent them out to begin their ministry. He included these precious words in verse 8: "Freely you have received, freely give." Adopt the attitude of Christ and give freely, with joy in your heart. He has given us so much. Our God is in the blessing business and, as His disciples, we must gladly make our blessings available to be used however He sees fit. Accept your responsibility and take Him at His word. The only way you can become happy in giving is to just *do it.* Take the challenge that the Lord offers to you, "Test me in this," says the Lord Almighty. This is one expectation that you must not ignore. Once you try Him in this sensitive area of your life, you will experience a change of heart. You will relinquish your status as a robber when you thoroughly understand and accept your God-given position of one who is *blessed* in order to be a blessing!

God Expects Forgiveness

My grandfather never thought that he would live past the age of sixty-two because eight of his siblings had suffered massive heart attacks and died at that age. When Grandpa reached and passed that ominous year, it was as if he had a new lease on life. Yet, heart disease caught up with him when he was sixty-seven. I was working in North Carolina in the respiratory intensive care unit when I received the call. It was 1979, and Grandpa had suffered a massive heart attack and was extremely close to death. So, I flew home in a gold Camaro rental car. I drove all those miles from North Carolina to Pennsylvania in the worst thunderstorm I had ever experienced. Tears were flowing down my face just as the streams of rain were flowing down from heaven.

My grandparents raised me. I was twelve years old when I went to live with them. Grandpa was more of a father to me than my biological father. He taught me how to drive, how to respect others, how to work hard and do a good job. It is his voice engraved in my heart with his sayings:

"Do it right, or don't do it at all."

"If you haven't anything good to say, say nothing at all."

I loved that man who had an eighth-grade education and never thought much of himself for he didn't read very well. He was the best mechanic in town and would give his shirt to anyone who needed one anytime of the day or night.

I safely arrived at the small community hospital on the hill. Grandpa was on IV drugs to maintain his blood pressure and could not talk due to his weakened condition and his being on strong analgesics for excruciating chest pain. However, he was awake enough to make desperate attempts to communicate a message that no one could decipher. His attempts to speak were jumbled ramblings, and his voice was so weak that he was only able to mouth the words. Grandpa had learned sign language at a young age for he had two brothers and one sister who were born deaf. So he tried constantly to sign his message, but no one else knew the sign language alphabet. The frustration of the family was tremendous. Visiting hours were only for ten-minute intervals every few hours because he was so critical. Everyone was so happy when I showed up, for I had the experience that they lacked. I worked with ventilator-dependent patients, and reading lips had become a skill that I had attained through years of ICU experience. My family wanted to know what was so vitally important to Grandpa when it seemed that his condition was deteriorating and death was near.

It was a heart-wrenching night, sitting in the waiting room of an old country hospital. While waiting for the ten-minute visiting time, the lights would dim and flicker. I came to understand why. Grandpa's heart would go into a life-threatening rhythm that required defibrillation. Each time they shocked him, the electrical surge would dim the waiting room lights. I kept that knowledge to myself. He was shocked more than thirteen times in a twenty-four hour period and I felt every one of them. I prayed so hard for this dear man whom I loved so much.

As the evening wore on, I began to figure out what Grandpa desperately wanted. He tried to write it, but his handwriting was illegible. Finally, I was able to read his lips. He wanted to see both of his kids. He was mouthing their names, DEE and BUD.

Grandpa wanted my mom and my Uncle Bud together in the same room. They'd had a falling out and had not spoken a word to each other for twelve years. Of course, they wanted me there to interpret so, next visiting time, the three of us went to Grandpa's bedside.

Mom was on his left and Uncle Bud was on his right. Grandpa reached up and took Mom's right hand and Bud's left hand and put them together. He then covered their hands with his own strong mechanic's hands and mouthed two words over and over, "Make up. Make up. Make up."

A father on the brink of death did not want to leave this earth knowing that his children did not have a right relationship with each other. Our Heavenly Father is no different. Christians are sons and daughters of God, and many times our relationships with one another are not what they should be. I believe it is time to makeup. We cannot allow the sinfulness of broken relationships and the attitude of an unforgiving spirit to dim our lights. Dare we consider what we are doing to our Heavenly Father's heart?

Forgiveness seems to be one of the hardest things that Christians and non-Christians are capable of doing with ease. Yet our faith and salvation is based upon the forgiveness applied to us through Christ's willingness to absorb every one of our sins into His own body. "If we confess our sin, he is faithful and just to forgive us our sins and to cleanse us from all unrighteousness" (1 John 1:9).

God is a forgiving God, and He strongly addresses in His Word that He expects us to be a forgiving people. His standards on this subject are direct and specific and are not open for debate. In Ephesians 4:32 the apostle Paul tells us to, "Be kind and compassionate one to another, forgiving each other. . . ." Then Paul gives us the *how to forgive model* as he continues, "Just as in Christ, God forgave you."

Colossians 3:13 says to "Bear with each other and forgive whatever grievances you may have against one another. Forgive as the Lord forgives you."

One day the Apostle Peter approached Christ and asked him a question about forgiveness.

"Lord, how many times shall I forgive my brother when he sins against me? Up to seven times?"

Jesus answered, "I tell you, not seven times, but seventy-seven times. Therefore, the kingdom of heaven is like a king who wanted to settle accounts with his servants. As he began the settlement, a man who owed him ten thousand talents was brought to him. Since he was not able to pay, the master ordered that he and his wife and his children and all that he had be sold to repay the debt. The servant fell on his knees before him. "Be patient with me, he begged, "and I will pay back everything." The servant's master took pity on him, canceled the debt and let him go.

But when that servant went out, he found one of his fellow servants who owed him a hundred denarii. He grabbed him and began to choke him. 'Pay back what you owe me!' he demanded.

His fellow servant fell to his knees and begged him, ' Be patient with me and I will pay you back.'

But he refused. Instead, he went off and had the man thrown into prison until he could pay the debt. When the other servants saw what had happened, they were greatly distressed and went and told their master everything that happened.

Then the master called the servant in. 'You wicked servant,' he said, 'I canceled all that debt of yours because you begged me to. Shouldn't you have had mercy on your fellow servant just as I had on you?' In anger his master turned him over to the jailers to be tortured, until he should pay back all he owed" (Matt.18:21-34).

Then in verse 35 Jesus makes this statement, "This is how my heavenly Father *will* treat each of you unless you forgive your brother from your heart" (*italics* added).

If we choose not to exercise forgiveness in our lives, the consequences are serious.

God promises us forgiveness in Matthew 6:14–15 "For if you forgive men when they sin against you, your heavenly Father *will* also forgive you. *But*, if you do not forgive men their sins, your Father *will not* forgive your sins" (*italics* added).

Matthew 11: 25 emphasizes this again: "And when you stand praying, if you hold anything against anyone, forgive him, so that your Father in heaven may forgive you your sins."

Can we examine these passages with open eyes and see the blazing convicting truth that God repeats over and over again? God promises us He will forgive us only if we adhere to His expectation to forgive those who sin against us. There is no question about God's expectations and His promise. If you withhold forgiveness from someone who has sinned against you, you are preventing God from forgiving you. In the eyes of God *grudge time* counts more heavily than *pew time*, tipping the scales hard into an area that is displeasing to God.

You can come to church every time the church doors are open. You can pray the most eloquent prayers, go to Bible studies, and generously give of your time and money to the Lord's work. However if you choose not to forgive, God will not forgive you. That is a scary promise, yet that is exactly what God says over and over again. Don't you want His forgiveness? Can't you see that this is one expectation you must meet wholeheartedly?

Why is forgiveness so vitally important? It is hard to forgive when someone has hurt or offended you. Yet the act of forgiving others provides the world with evidence that Christianity is alive. Forgiveness identifies Christ at work within His believers. Forgiveness stands out. It is not a natural response; it is a supernatural response that is only possible when we consider the enormous amount of sin that God forgave from each of our lives.

Once I sat in an airport waiting for a delayed plane. It was extremely close quarters. I was knitting and traveling alone. I didn't mean to eavesdrop, but two businessmen were talking very loudly, and I could not help but hear this sad story. One man was discussing his daughter. Apparently she had been quite a rebel in her teenage years and had hurt her father often in a variety of ways. He was fed up with her. Her disobedience and disrespect had chopped away at any feelings of love he had toward her. He told his friend that he hadn't spoken to her in many years now and truly was relieved. His last statement shocked me. He said, "To be honest, I wouldn't care if she was dead."

I prayed for that man and his relationship with his daughter. When I consider the multiple times I have broken the heart of my Heavenly Father by doing things that were disgusting in His sight, I can't imagine what I would have ever done if God gave up on me. Yet, today, I see broken relationships from people who refuse to forgive: patients' families, as well as, those who are in the family of God. Refusing to forgive others is a dangerous practice because *God never intended relationships to be disposable.* How can we try to draw someone to God by saying that He desires a personal relationship with each of us when we refuse to place value on the relationships within our own lives?

I remembered and prayed for that airport businessman again one night while I was at work. I was in ICU and there was a patient that was extremely unstable. Whenever a patient is critical, patient visitation is denied for all. I had finished starting two IV's on this particular patient and was charting when the visitor phone rang. All the other nurses were with the doctors helping with the unstable patient, so I answered the phone. A young woman was inquiring about her father in room 8. Her name was Kathy, and she wanted to see him as soon as it was possible. I informed her of the situation and assured her that we would do what we could to let her visit her dad. I told her that I would check on him and let him know that she was in the waiting room.

I then went into room 8, introduced myself, asked this man how he was doing and told him that Kathy, his daughter was in the waiting room. I then asked him if there was anything that I could do for him, and he asked me to bring him a glass of ice water. When I returned with the water, he asked me this question, "Are you sure she said 'Kathy'?"

My answer was, "Yes, I do believe so." Then I asked him, "Do you have a daughter by that name?"

"Well yes," was his reply, "but I haven't seen her for seven years. Please do anything that you can to let her in to see me."

I cleared it with the nurses in charge. I closed all the drapes and doors around the critical patient and went to the waiting room. I found Kathy and brought her to her father's bedside. Hopefully, hearts were being mended in room 8. As I walked out of the ICU, I sent up a prayer for the airport dad and his daughter. It was short and to the point: *Lord, please don't let that man wait until he has a heart attack, too.* Take heed of my grandfather's advice and makeup. There is no better time than now. Remember, forgiveness results in reconciliation. Forgive just as God through Christ forgave you. Godly forgiveness is intertwined with forgetfulness as he assures us in Isaiah 43:25: "I, even I, am he who blots out your transgressions, for my own sake, and remembers your sins no more."

If you are having trouble in this area of your life, remember Christ's story about the men that owed so much debt and realize that the Lord was talking about us. If God through Christ can forgive us so much, how dare we not forgive when someone sins against us? Our debt was paid in full by the only one who had money in the bank. When Adam fell, we all became spiritually bankrupt. So when someone sins against you or your loved ones, consider these thoughts:

If my debt and sins against Christ are forgiven me, then I need to emulate Christ and forgive others.

If there is no such thing as a disposable relationship in the eyes of God, then I need to value my relationships with others just as God values His relationship with me.

Any sinful act towards me is miniscule in comparison to the sins that bombarded Christ. If He can forgive, He can teach me to forgive if I am willing to learn.

Bitterness and resentment are the fruit that comes from a heart that will not forgive. Christ has no part of that kind of fruit.

There is no sin so great that Christ's forgiveness cannot reach, engulf, and vaporize.

In the Gospel of John 1:29, John the Baptist looked up and saw Jesus approaching and He exclaimed, "Look, the Lamb of God, who takes away the sins of the world."

There isn't a sin that He can't forgive, for He came to take them all. We must meet God's expectations for forgiveness that He taught us in His prayer. Remember? "Forgive us our debts as we forgive our debtors" (Matt. 6:12). Let us hold to God's standard of forgiveness and live with the assurance of the beautiful promise that is connected to it. The promise is found in Luke 6:37 "Forgive and you *will be* forgiven!" (*italics* added).

God Expects Love

As Christians we always have the capacity to grow in our faith as we search the Word to know God on a deeper level. We can dig deeper and find meaning in scripture passages we have read many times in our lives that thrill our soul, as we learn to let God's Word sink into our minds and hearts. This chapter on expectations and promises has blessed me tremendously. As we endeavor to explore love and obedience and relate them to what God expects. Not wanting to miss one point, I turned in my Bible to James 1:5 to ask God for wisdom as I prepare this chapter. I found another precious promise:

If any of you lacks wisdom, he should ask God, who gives generously to all without finding fault, and *it will* be given to him.

But when he asks, he must believe and not doubt, because

he who doubts is like a wave of the sea, blown and tossed by the wind (*italics* added).

We all need wisdom from God to examine this subject matter. I believe strongly that honor and forgiveness are definite expectations of our God that have positive or negative outcomes depending upon our personal choices. Then I considered these questions, "Can anyone expect to be loved? Does God *expect* us to love Him?" I believe the answer is yes. God not only expects us to love Him, He expects our love to be saturated with obedience.

Jesus was approached by a teacher of the law in Mark 12:28. He posed this question:

> "Of all the commandments, which is the most important?"
> "The most important one," answered Jesus, "is this: 'Hear, O Israel, the Lord our God, the Lord is one. Love the Lord your God with all your heart and with all your soul and with all your mind and with all your strength!'
> The second is this: 'Love your neighbor as yourself.' There is no commandment greater than these."

Now look closely at the teacher's response to Christ's answer.

> "Well said, teacher," the man replied. "You are right in saying that God is one and there is no other but him. To love him with all your heart, with all your understanding and with all your strength and to love your neighbor as yourself is more important than all burnt offerings and sacrifices. When Jesus saw that he had answered wisely, he said to him, "You are not far from the Kingdom of God" (Mark 12:32-33).

In reference to the greatest commandment, Jesus referred back to Deuteronomy 5 and 6 where Moses was expounding on the laws given to him directly by God. Before we are told to love God, a preliminary truth is exclaimed in the Old and New Testaments alike. The Lord our God is one. This accents the total uniqueness and position of God.

God and God alone, "There is no other" is the paraphrase the teacher used to describe this statement. Then the command is given to love Him, the one and only God.

Consider the word *command*. It can be defined as an authoritative directive or order (*Webster II New College Dictionary*). Jesus used the word command not only in regards to loving his Father, but also when he discussed love for one another.

> "My command is this: Love each other as I have loved you" (John 15:12).

> "This is my command love each other" (John 15:17).

When we receive commands from God the Father and Jesus, His Son, I believe we are expected to follow their directive.

When a sergeant in the military gives a specific command to a private, the sergeant expects the private to follow through with his request. However, we are not programmable robots; we are humans with the freedom of choice. To follow, or not to follow, are the two choices that the private faces. If he chooses to follow and do exactly what is required of him, his action makes several statements:

- He has respect for the sergeant.
- He is trustworthy.
- He sees his own position as important. He does his part no matter how small.
- He is faithful and can follow through with his assignments.

If the private chooses not to follow the sergeant's command, the message sent by this private's decision has extremely negative results.

- In the eyes of the private, the sergeant's rank is meaningless.
- A mission may be placed in danger.
- Other lives may be thrown into harm's way.
- When a command is given and disregarded, there will be consequences attached to this decision.

So how do we want to deal with the commands of God? Moses gave us some good advice: "So be careful to do what the Lord your God has commanded you; do not turn aside to the right or to the left. Walk in all the way that the Lord your God has commanded you, so that you may prosper and prolong your days in the land that you will possess" (Deut. 5:35).

When Jesus said the greatest command is to love the Lord, He prefaced the command with a reminder of the rank and position of God. When I was thinking about the highest military rank, I asked my husband if a Five Star General was the highest-ranking officer. He reminded me that the President of the United States was the Commander and Chief. So when I think of the rank of God, I love the title, "Most High."

In Genesis 14:18-20, Melchizidek gave a blessing to Abram and God:

"Blessed be Abram by God *Most High*, Creator of heaven and earth. And blessed be God *Most High*, who delivered your enemies into your hands" (*Italics* mine).

In Mark 5:7 Jesus encounters a man possessed and we see that even demons know the rank of God and Christ. He shouted at the top of his voice, "What do you want with me, Jesus, Son of the *Most High* God?" (*Italics* mine).

Most High means there is no one higher. So when the Most High God gives us a command, I believe He expects us to follow. When the Most High speaks, He deserves our full attention. When He gives us a command, He provides detailed instructions and illustrations of successful maneuvers by others under His command. Under His guidance we are able to follow through with whatever He requests. His command: "Love me." He continues, "Let me show you how:

• With all of your heart
• With all of your soul
• With all of your mind
• With all of your strength.
• And love others: love your neighbor as yourself."

When we look at the love that God desires from us, we can summarize that God wants a love that is a total commitment. The Most High wants us to love Him *with all.*

- Halfhearted love is insufficient.
- Holding onto your own will, emotions, and seclusion of your innermost self will only hinder God's command.
- An uncontrolled thought life won't cut it.
- A weak, unexercised, unused love will always miss the mark.

Love for God is not a compartmentalized love. Let me explain that concept by using the medical profession as an example. Many years ago one physician would take care of patients from birth to death. Today, you may be admitted to the cardiac unit with chest pain. Your physician will consult a cardiologist to manage your heart concerns. Your lab results may reveal your kidneys are in failure. A kidney specialist may be consulted. Then one morning your stomach is in distress, and another physician is consulted whose focus is gastrointestinal problems. You have one physical body that has become compartmentalized into heart, kidney, and stomach. Each specialist will focus on his area of expertise. They will find your problem, and you will receive treatment and hopefully return to health.

God does not want compartmentalized love from us. We cannot attend church or sing in the choir and go home and watch trash on TV. We shouldn't teach Bible study if we detest some of those attending the class. We cannot love God only during Sunday worship and then neglect Him and His Word the rest of the week. Our love for Him must encompass *all* that we are, at all times.

Our love for Him must be with a heart of complete devotion.

Our love for Him must captivate our thinking.

Our love for Him must be intentional and have stamina and endurance.

Our love for Him must include the invisible, living unique part of each of us: we must love Him with our essence, our being, our life.

God expects us to love Him completely with all, not part, not some, but *with all.* We can summarize this section with this statement. When it comes to love, the Most High expects nothing less than *all.*

This entire subject of Christians loving God brings out a lot of questions to think about. Do you think that through the years our concentration has been more focused on *God's love toward us* instead of our love toward God? Look at your own life and check out the balance of your love.

I need to share with you a God-moment that helped me to love God better than I had ever loved Him. I have one son. His name is Will, and if you have a child or children you understand the love a parent feels. From the time that Will could understand, I made a point to tell him things that he could keep in his little heart and mind so that he would always know he was accepted and loved. I would tell him, "William, I'm so glad you are mine. If God would have let me into a room full of little boys and allowed me to pick one, I could never have picked a sweeter boy than the one He gave me."

I also wanted to instill in my son, how much God loved him. So I would tell him, "William, I love you so much. But always remember God loves you more."

One day when I was reading my Bible, I came across a passage that changed my love for the Most High God.

Jesus is speaking, "As the Father has loved me, so have I loved you" (John 15:9).

God loved Jesus. He was His Father. He saw His birth. He saw Him cut His first tooth. He saw His first steps, His first skinned knee. God loved His only son. He let Him know He loved him. God told him, "I'm so glad You're mine."

As soon as Jesus was baptized, He went up out of the water. At that moment heaven was opened, and He saw the Spirit of God descending like a dove and lighting on Him. And a voice from heaven said, "This is my Son, whom I love; with him I am well pleased" (Matt. 3:16).

God loved His Son. God loved us. God gave Jesus, His one and only Son. He loved Him just like I love Will, possibly more than I am capable of loving. Some questions won't be answered until we get to heaven, but I have wondered how God handled the cross. He could not look upon sin, yet Christ became sin. So what held God's eyes that day? Do you think that He might have been looking at us? I have wondered if He knew how many of us would choose to love Him back, and if our future love for God in Christ could possibly have given comfort to the broken heart of the Most High God. So often we focus on the physical pain of Jesus, yet His Father must have suffered also. Our God is a God of deep emotion. He loved His Son so much. Yet He was able to let Him suffer and die for one reason and only one reason. YOU and ME—He loves us, too.

Any human heart cannot begin to measure the greatness of the love our God is capable of expressing. So what is your response when you consider God's command, "Love me with *all* your heart?" Personally, I just can't help myself. When I consider His rank and position and His experience, I have a desire within me to meet this expectation. I so want to love Him well, for He has loved me completely for so long. There is an old hymn entitled, "O Love That Will Not Let Me Go." When you consider the heart of God, His love will not let you go and this command will be your greatest Joy to follow without hesitation. Love God with *all* and be complete in Him.

"And so we know and rely on the love God has for us. God is love. Whoever lives in love lives in God, and God in him. In this way love is made complete among us so that we will have confidence on the Day of Judgment, because in this world we are like him" (1 John 4:16-17).

The second part of the greatest commandment Jesus added is "to love your neighbor as yourself." In Luke 10:25-37, an expert of the law stood up and inquired of Jesus what the requirements for heaven were. Jesus answered him with the greatest commandment and added the above phrase. The expert then posed this question,

"And who is my neighbor?"

In reply Jesus said:

> "A man was going down from Jerusalem to Jericho, when he fell into the hands of robbers. They stripped him of his clothes, beat him and went away, leaving him half dead. A priest happened to be going down the same road, and when he saw the man, he passed by on the other side. So too, a Levite, when he came to the place and saw him, passed by on the other side. But a Samaritan, as he traveled, came where the man was; and when he saw him, he took pity on him. He went to him and bandaged his wounds, pouring on oil and

wine. Then he put the man on his own donkey, took him to an inn and took care of him. The next day he took out two silver coins and gave them to the innkeeper. 'Look after him,' he said, 'and when I return, I will reimburse you for any extra expense you may have.'

"Which of these three do you think was a neighbor to the man who fell into the hands of robbers?" The expert in the law replied, "The one who had mercy on him." Jesus told him, "Go and do likewise."

Love never should be locked up behind the doors of the church. We are called to see and meet the needs of those around us. In our world, the needs of our neighbors are tremendous, and we should be grateful that ministries exist to help reach the needy of our world. We don't need to know the ones that we help. Mercy expects nothing in return. Micah 6: 8 is a wonderful verse that supports this concept well:

He has showed you, O man, what is good.
And what the Lord requires of You?
To act justly and to love mercy
And to walk humbly with your God.

Love for God and love for others are commands that Christ and His Father directed to us. However, we cannot ignore the consistent emphasis on obedience. If we are aware of God's stance on love and yet do not heed His instructions on how to live the life He models, our knowledge alone is totally meaningless. Let me give an example in order to clarify this point:

I worked with the sweetest nurse for many years. Her husband was an alcoholic and she was an enabler. She read every book ever printed on the subject of alcoholism and codependency. She could explain the subject matter, give advice to others, and even evaluate her own situation. One day while discussing her life, she made this statement, "I know what I am supposed to do, and I understand codependency completely. If only I could take the knowledge that I have and put it into action. It isn't a matter of not knowing, it is simply a lack of application."

The place where the knowledge of love and action meet can be called the "Land of Obedience."

"If you love me, you will *obey* what I command" (John 14:15, *italics* added).

"Whoever has my commands and *obeys* them, he is the one who loves me. He who loves me will be loved by my Father, and I too will love him and show myself to him" (John 14:21, *italics* added).

"If anyone loves me, he will *obey* my teaching. My Father will love him, and we will come to him and make our home with him. He who does not love me will *not obey* my teaching" (John 14:23, *italics* added).

"We know that we have come to know him if we *obey* his commands. The man who says, "I know him, but does not do what he commands is a liar and the truth is not in him. But if anyone *obeys* his word, God's love is truly made complete in him" (I John 2:3, *italics* added).

The above scriptures illustrate the direct connection between love and obedience. In Corinthians 9:13 Paul is addressing the Corinthian church: "Because of the service by which you have proved yourselves, men will praise God for the obedience that accompanies your confession of the gospel of Christ. . . ."

What accompanies their confession of the gospel? Obedience, and their acts of obedience have proved them to be servants of Christ. Obedience intertwined with love gives the world evidence of the Gospel of Christ. Love defined in 2 John 1:6 suggests that love and obedience are inseparable.

"And this is love; that we walk in obedience to His commands. As you have heard from the beginning, His command is that you walk in love."

We only walk through this life once. If we choose to walk the road of life with God, we must walk in obedience to His commands in order to be blessings and live our lives wanting to be available to bless the lives of those in need. May we adopt a forgiving spirit and never forget that forgiveness shouts that you value relationships with others just as much as Jesus does. And last but not least, walk a life of love soaked with obedience and remember the One who walked the path to Golgotha.

"For just as through the disobedience of the one man *the many* were made sinners, so also through the obedience of one man *the many* will be made righteous" (Romans 5:19, *italics* added).

So may we, who are included in *the many*, "live a life of love, just as Christ loved us and gave himself up for us as a fragrant offering and sacrifice to God" (Eph. 5:2). Let us meet this expectation with the recognition that the One who has given the command has also given us the promise. Love and obey the Most High and hold to the truth of 1 Kings 8:23:

"Oh Lord, God of Israel, there is no God like you in heaven above or on earth below—You who keep your covenant of love with your servants who continue wholeheartedly in your way."

I have but one life that God has entrusted to me. When I think that Christ only lived on earth in human form for thirty-three years, I often look at how old I am. Then I ask him, "Lord, am I doing enough? Am I living up to Your expectations for this one and only life?" I know that Jesus has been given the authority to judge us or place our lives in a scale and weigh the actions of our lives and the motives of our hearts. I don't want to wait until my life is over for this process to take place. I want to "weigh-in" on a regular basis in order to receive an honest evaluation so that I can make any necessary adjustments to my life while I am still walking about in my earth-suit.

So I challenge you to do the same. Ask yourself, "Am I living up to the expectations of God?" The four areas of honor, giving, forgiving and loving in obedience are very intimate areas to examine. I believe they are extremely important. Please be aware that this list was never meant to be a complete representation of all the expectations of God. However, if we are to contemplate the truths we have covered in the various scriptures we have read, our lives will definitely change. There is nothing more wonderful than holding onto the promises of God. As He has repeated over and over again to us, *"I will,"* perhaps we should follow His lead and give him the following response: "Lord, I *will* honor, I *will* give, I *will* forgive, I *will* love, I *will* obey. *I promise.* Amen."

6. The Whatever Principle

IN LIFE WE ENCOUNTER SITUATIONS that influence our decisions, build our character, and stretch our faith. When I examine my own life experiences, I realize that positive and negative circumstances contribute to the person that I am becoming. Whenever critical incidents have blown up a secure bridge or highway along the journey of my life, the detour has always provided a much greater portion of wisdom, knowledge, and insight.

After a crisis, examination of the circumstances can reveal benefits and valuable life lessons that are etched forever into our hearts and memories. As I write this chapter, Hurricane Katrina has left her mark. Katrina slammed into the lives of so many precious people destroying safety, security, and the inner peace of all who love humanity. If humans had the power to turn back time and evacuate every home at risk in Katrina's angry path, we would snap our fingers and do just that. We would prevent the casualties of 9/11, as well as protect and cradle all those hit by the mountain of water named "tsunami." If we could… we would… but we can't. We cannot prevent a neighbor from having a massive heart attack. We cannot remove the pain and anger of parents when their teenage daughter is murdered in their own home.

If we could pick and choose life circumstances, many, if not all people, would want to pick only the pleasant situations that result in happy endings. Then what would we do with the pain? If there would be some means to dispose of all the heartbreaking things that occur in our lives, how could we do this?

What if each of us could gather up all the negative experiences of our lives and place pictures, trinkets, and memorabilia in dark storage boxes and deliver them to a huge warehouse in a remote part of a desert? The shelves and aisles would all be categorized and our boxes stacked accordingly. The number of different categories in this warehouse would cover quite an assortment of painful life experiences. Each box could be given a value or number to represent the degree of pain evoked. However, *perception of pain belongs totally to the individual subjected to the trauma, whether the pain is physical, mental, emotional, or spiritual.*

My pain is mine alone. Your pain belongs to you. Yet the etiology or cause of our pain may come from the same source. So the aisles in the warehouse would be labeled with pain producers so familiar to so many: natural disaster, rape, downsizing, death, debt, divorce, cancer, lies, bankruptcy, abortion, dementia, mental illness, physical impairment, and false accusation.

This list is not conclusive, but it is sufficient to arrive at a most important point. Do you see the common ingredient of pain? I believe it is *loss*. Sometimes it is a major or minor loss, but sometimes one circumstance can deal a life several losses all at once.

Pretend you know a twelve-year-old girl whose parents have divorced. She has a divorce box to take to the "unload your losses" warehouse. In her divorce box, this child has placed a picture of her house. Often children of divorce are removed from their homes and are placed in the custody of a foster home, grandparents, aunts and uncles, or other relatives. This twelve-year-old may never return home again. She is very familiar with displacement. Then you see pictures of her brothers and sisters and neighborhood friends. Not only does displacement physically remove a child from familiar surroundings, but sometimes it also severs relationships with friends and family members. Then you see a dog collar, and you surmise that the dog went to live with someone else. Another loss. Then you spy the tennis ball beside the pair of satin toe shoes, and you realize that you are looking at the loss of dreams. A young child may love tennis, basketball, ballet, or soccer and be moved to a town where none of these activities are available or, even if they are, the divorce may have ended the funding for such. This is just one fictitious sampling of one loss box packed full of pain from a twelve-year-old. Think of the number of divorces in our country and imagine the different possible contents from abuse to neglect. This aisle must be very long and the shelves quite sturdy.

Imagine the miles of boxes stacked in the death aisle. Life is but a vapor that appears for a little while then vanishes away. We all will die a physical death and not one of us is exempt nor do we get to choose the method. The death aisle contains a tremendous amount of pain from sudden infant death syndrome to suicide and murder. Of course for some, the degree of pain that death brings can be intertwined with joy if the person had been suffering or was longing for heaven.

Yet for some the loss of a loved one is so great that they would never contemplate bringing their box to the warehouse. They cling to their box with all the pain, and sometimes they crawl into that box and cover themselves with the lid. They become so consumed with the events surrounding the loss of their loved one that they become terribly depressed or angry and are unable to function in the world. Some dear people spend so much time in the dark box that when, and if they come out, they are blinded by the light and cannot see the love and needs of others in their lives. They become unable to receive love, and, in some cases, anger can become the only emotion they are capable of expressing. Loving simply hurts too much when a loved one dies, so they decide never to love again. This is a great defense against pain and many will adopt this mechanism and spend the rest of their lives covered in anger, numbness, or a state of emotional paralysis.

We can only surmise the pain and stories in each death box. I will never forget a conversation I had with a sweet elderly patient. We talked about our families and discovered we both had one son. Her son was dead. When I asked her how it happened, she explained that he was in his early thirties, and he had a job that required traveling. While sleeping in a hotel room in St. Louis, he was robbed and murdered for about $40. Her son's killer was never found. Tucked inside this woman's box, labeled with the death of her son, is the additional loss of closure.

Loss surrounds us. Loss touches us all. Loss is personal. Loss comes with different degrees of individual significance.

I have a dear friend who has had several jobs due to company mergers, downsizing, and shutdowns. You and I might think that another job loss would be absolutely devastating to him. Surprise. If this man lost his job again, he more than likely would not be shaken, for with every job loss in his life, he went job hunting. Each time he landed a better job with better benefits and better pay. He now realizes that he would never have looked for any of these jobs if he were not forced to do so. His job loss box would be a "lightweight" in comparison to other losses in his life!

In reality, we cannot pack our pain into a box and stack it in a secluded desert warehouse. We cannot unload our losses and live as if they have never happened. If we attempt to do that, we are living in denial. That choice does not produce a healthy life. So what can we do with the pain and the losses in life? If coping were as tangible as a chocolate bar and you loved chocolate, I'd break you off a big piece—a chunk! So I am offering you a huge chunk of *cope*. I hope that even a morsel or a taste of the following truths can offer you sincere help when you are heartbroken and feel as though there is no more sweetness in life for you.

1. Loss has no respect for person, social status, or time.

The rain falls on the just and the unjust. We must realize that loss and pain are familiar to all who live in this world. There is no exception. Painful loss crosses racial divides, generation gaps, and religious and political differences.

2. Pain and loss are powerful change agents.

Remember the story of Kelly in the chapter titled "My Paul Harvey God" who lost her husband? Her loss filled her with a desire to help others so she achieved a certificate in grief counseling from the bereavement academy. Her pain changed the direction in her life. Often support groups rely on the common ground of pain to reach out and encourage one another in order to change. Such groups utilize accountability and encouragement in order to achieve common goals that result in changed lives when one is alcoholic, drug addicted, or abused. Changes can also occur in systems, such as air travel after 9/11. Before that tragedy we never had to take off our tennis shoes or be frisked before boarding a plane. Now it is common practice. Change happens, and often pain and loss can be the catalyst.

3. We each need our pain.

If there really were a place to unload losses and walk away as if sad things never happened, we would have to leave all of our memories behind. Where there is great love, there is great pain. With every tear we shed, a precious memory seems to be connected. Sometimes things stimulate our senses and bring back memories that are so dear. It only takes the smell of peonies in the spring for me to remember Grandma. She always floated a bowl of them on the dining room table. When we remember someone's life or share precious moments of his or her life with others, we are signifying that that life had relevance and always will. We make memories, and we treasure memories. At the Last Supper the Lord set the precedence for Communion and said, "Do this in remembrance of me." Remembering is healing and has the ability to comfort and sustain.

There is another very important reason that we should not ignore our life losses. We may need to share survival tips with friends experiencing the same kinds of pains we know too well. Our experience dealing with pain and loss can give another person hope. Pain has tremendous purpose, especially shared pain.

4. God can use pain and loss for your own good and protection.

This is an extremely important concept to consider when the wounds are fresh and tender. We don't have the foresight of God. Yet he gives us an absolute in Romans 8:28:

"And we know that in all things God works for the good of those who love him, who have been called according to his purpose."

In *all* things God is working for our good, not just in some situations, but in *all* situations. At times this is hard for us to believe, but let's examine a painful time in one man's life and see just how this scripture applies.

Any Man's Terror

When the men approached Harold's office door, he had no clue where the conversation would lead. Their faces were strained and troubled and after awkward small talk, they entered his office and found seats around his desk. The reason for the meeting quickly spilled out.

"Harold," they began, "there is a very serious situation that has come to our attention. We cannot reveal details. The only thing that we can tell you is that you have been accused, and an investigation has begun."

So began the terror.

Harold, a faithful and devoted Christian, was married to a lovely woman who was in charge of Sunday school and Christian education at their church. This devoted couple spent their weekends and free time investing in the lives of troubled youth. They had taught, fed, loved, and led many to Jesus. They had tithed and used bonus monies to help others for years.

Accused. The most heart-wrenching part of this situation was that Harold had to go home and face the wife he adored and tell her that he was being investigated but was not sure why. He felt certain that he would be fired. Having worked for this company for over ten years, he had acquired a great deal of company stock which at this time he decided to liquidate and reinvest elsewhere. He sold all his stock at a very good price and was prepared to walk away from the company. For several weeks, Harold and his wife lived in limbo.

After about six weeks, the management met with Harold once again. They revealed that one of his staff had charged him with inappropriate behavior and harassment. He had had a meeting with his secretary and was reported to have given her this ultimatum: "Have dinner with me or you won't receive a good evaluation."

Harold was a thorough man, and he had documented the topics, objectives, and goals for that entire meeting. He was able to provide the investigating team with the outlines and details of their conversation. The case was dropped, and the woman was moved to another area of the company to work for a different manager. Harold never readjusted his investments. It wasn't long after this incident that the company began to experience problems, and the stock fell drastically. In retrospect, Harold is very thankful for those terrible weeks in his life when he was falsely accused for something that he would never dream of doing. The loss of peace during that time motivated him to move his money. He sees this situation as something that God used to preserve his financial future.

Let us review the four points of pain and loss and see how they apply to Harold's experience.

1. Loss has no respect for person, social status or time.

Harold and his wife tithed and loved to serve the Lord. Note this extremely important fact. Christians are not exempt from pain. We are sometimes the prime targets for false accusations, lies, and evil schemes.

2. Pain and loss are powerful change agents.

Think of a different scenario. What if the accusation had never happened? Harold would never have had a reason to move his funds. His financial losses would have been great. Being the generous people of God that they are, this scenario would have diminished their capacity to support God's work. In many ways, God protected His own investment, for he knows the very heart of this couple so well.

3. We each need our pain.

There are two points that fall under this principle. First, if there is ever a friend or fellow worker who is in the same situation, Harold can provide support and encouragement. He is familiar with this pain, and he now has the experience and empathy to help another man deal with this tragic situation.

Harold's ability to trust God has increased due to this painful experience. Pain has a tendency to draw us closer to God and makes us more pliable and more dependent. Pain causes us to put our faith into action. Exercised faith speaks volumes.

4. God can use pain and loss for our own good and protection.

Harold and his wife can now embrace Romans 8:28 and realize that God has given them a personal, tangible scenario to remember and share in order to reinforce the fact that God indeed works in our lives for our good! God alone can see the future, and he alone can use or manipulate whatever means available to cause us to act, therefore keeping any part of our lives safe.

We have taken a broad view of many of the situations that elicit pain and loss in the life of any individual. We can draw the conclusion that many different people share the same personal losses. If we examine the response to any acute or sudden distressing situation, we definitely establish yet another commonality. Usually a three-letter word is repeated over and over and over again. "Why? Why me? Why Lord? Why my house? Why my family? Lord, why did You let this happen? Why didn't You prevent this? Lord, if You love me, why are You doing this to me?"

Some people will focus on these questions for the rest of their lives. Some will be defeated by their tragedy and will never be able to crawl out of the pit of shock or grief. Then there are some individuals who scream out their questions while in agony and pain and plead their case before their God expecting him to not only hear them, but to clearly answer them. These driven people will be the ones who will be able to contemplate the hand of God at work in their heartache.

How do you feel about questioning God? Some feel it is inappropriate for people to question the Almighty, yet when we check out Scripture we find that God is more than receptive to our inquiries. Look at how the minor prophet Habakkuk questioned God in Habakkuk 1:2-4 when he and his people were living in a stressful situation that was beyond their capacity to understand. He began his inquiry, "How long, O Lord, must I call for help, but you do not listen? Or cry out to you Violence! But you do not save? Why do you make me look at injustice? Why do you tolerate wrong? Destruction and violence are before me; there is strife, and conflict abounds. Therefore the law is paralyzed and justice is perverted."

God answered: "Look at the nations and watch and be utterly amazed. For I am going to do something in your days that you would not believe even if you were told."

God Is Always at Work, Doing Something Unbelievable.

We must trust that God remains calm and in total control at all times. He can see the future; we can't, so we must rely on God's leading, for essentially we are blind. God can use the very things that seem unbearable to us in an extremely beneficial manner for individuals or the entire nation. Could God possibly use a tragedy such as Katrina to unite our nation with compassion, prayer, and a tremendous continual outpouring of generosity to its victims? Could the fact that those families were not rescued as rapidly as we all desired be God's way of pulling hard at our human heart strings, thus loosening the purse strings of many? Remember God's view is greater than ours.

There were many heroes of this tragedy that showed unconditional love by taking families into their own homes and welcoming strangers into their communities and schools with open arms. The disaster and rescue teams worked tirelessly with one common mission—to save as many lives as they possibly could. Do you realize that with each life saved, the bus drivers, helicopter pilots, army soldiers, and national guardsmen put their own lives at risk, for I doubt they had much sleep or food during their rescue efforts? Great love and compassion has been unleashed in our country, and the cause of this response is due to the great extent of pain and loss of our brothers and sisters. God is always awake, alert, and working.

When we question the Lord, He answers us with the reassurance that He will never abandon us. He instructs us to keep our eyes open. "Look" to be observant of the situation "Watch" and "Be Utterly Amazed" at His work and His intervention. We have already established the fact that pain and loss strikes our lives without any regard or respect to person, status, or timing. Preparation is everything. Yet when we are faced with a tragedy or personal crisis, we often lose all ability to cope. We need to be better prepared. The best preparation I know is a sincere commitment to live each day by "The Whatever Principle." This life-changing principle is presented in the book of Daniel by three Godly men and a misdirected king.

King Nebuchadnezzar made a huge image of gold and issued a command that all people would fall down and worship this idol whenever they heard a musical instrument. Daniel had three friends that loved God. They did not respond to the King's command, and their disrespect was reported. The king then summoned these men and told them:

"Now when you hear the sound of the horn, flute, zither, lyre, harp, pipes and all kinds of music if you are ready to fall down and worship the image I made, very good. But if you do not worship it, you will be thrown immediately into a blazing furnace. Then what god will be able to rescue you from my hand?"

Shadrach, Meshach and Abednego replied to the king, "O Nebuchadnezzar, we do not need to defend ourselves before you in this matter. If we are thrown into the blazing furnace, the God we serve *is able to save us from it,* and he will rescue us from your hand, O king. *But even if he does not,* we want you to know O king, that we will not serve your gods or worship the image of gold you have set up" (Dan. 3:15-27, *italics* added).

So the king became livid and turned the furnace seven times hotter than normal. He had his soldiers bind the three God-fearing men, and they were thrown into the flames. However, the king kept watching, and he was astonished at what his eyes beheld. He questioned the advisers, "Weren't there three men that we tied up and threw into the fire?" They replied, "Certainly, O king." He said, "Look! I see four men walking around in the fire, unbound and unharmed, and the fourth looks like a son of the gods." Nebuchadnezzar then approached the opening of the blazing furnace and shouted, "Shadrach, Meshach and Abednego, servants of the Most High God, come out! Come here!"

And they did, without a hair singed or even the smell of smoke on their body or clothing.

Sometimes in our lives, when we are in the furnace, we approach our Heavenly Father with the following barrage of questions and confusion: "Lord, what have I ever done to deserve this? Haven't I been faithful to you? I have served you for many years. I have openly confessed my faith in you without shame. I am your child. What are you thinking? What are you doing to me?"

That is a response that we could potentially place before our God. Look closely at the focus of these questions. Who is the person in the limelight? Look at the pronouns and we repeatedly see "I" and "me." The concentration is on self, and the person is gazing intently at the deadly flames and in a subtle way placing the blame and responsibility for the whole situation on God. This attitude of the human heart and mind reeks of a familiar "garden gimmick" don't you agree?

More than likely you have seen or heard the following scene sometime in your life. Just yesterday a man at work was describing his family situation. His dad suffers from Alzheimer's disease and is now living in a nursing home. His mother has chosen bitterness and anger as her closest companions. Where does she direct her anger? She is mad at God for doing this to her. Her son and his pastor have tried so hard to reason with her to no avail.

Could Shadrach, Meshach, and Abednego have been angry with God for putting them in such a *hot* situation? Sure, but they never once asked even one question, nor did they blame God for their plight. Why not? Because I believe that their focus was never on themselves or even on the flames. Their focus was on their God. Here is another marvelous story of a man with proper focus. The story is found in the daily devotional entitled *Streams in the Desert:*

I went to America some years ago with the captain of a steamer, who was a very devoted Christian. When off the coast of Newfoundland he said to me, "The last time I crossed here, five weeks ago, something happened which revolutionized the whole of my Christian life. We had George Mueller of Bristol on board. I had been on the bridge twenty-four hours and never left it. George Mueller came to me, and said, "Captain, I have come to tell you that I must be in Quebec Saturday afternoon."

"It is impossible," I said.

"Very well, if your ship cannot take me, God will find some other way. I have never broken an engagement for fifty-seven years. Let us go down into the chartroom and pray." I looked at that man of God, and thought to myself, what lunatic asylum can that man have come from? I never heard of such a thing as this. "Mr. Mueller," I said, "do you know how dense this fog is?" "No," he replied, "*my eye is not on the density of the fog, but on the living God, who controls every circumstance of my life.*"

He knelt down and prayed one of the most simple prayers, and when he had finished I was going to pray: but he put his hand on my shoulder, and told me *not* to pray.

"First, you do not believe he will answer; and second I believe he already has, and there is no need whatever for you to pray about it."

I looked at him, and he said, "Captain, I have known my Lord for fifty-seven years, and there has never been a single day that I have failed to get audience with the King. Get up Captain and open the door, and you will find the fog gone." I got up and the fog was indeed gone. On Saturday afternoon George Mueller was in Quebec for his engagement.

Just as George was not looking at the fog, the three men were not looking at the flames, but to the God they knew and loved so deeply. Shadrach, Meshach, and Abednego would never be willing to transfer their allegiance or worship any other.

These men provide us with a tremendous lesson: *When faced with adversity in your life, take your eyes off yourself and the situation and keep your heart and mind completely focused upon God.*

It seems as though some people cannot break away from the old school mentality that in the event that trouble appears in a person's life, it is the deserved result of some terrible action, thought, or deed. If you have problems, some believe you must have sinned badly, and this is your punishment. True, sin does definitely have consequences. But I believe that we have the tendency at times to take full possession of circumstances that don't belong to us at all. We use the Christian jargon, "my faith is being tested." I am sure that in every Christian life there will be trials, tests, and even persecution for some.

However, there are times that God can use His people as instruments for a test that belongs to someone else. Shadrach, Meshach, and Abednego loved the Lord, and their faith was secure. With careful scrutiny of the story, we can surmise that their faith was absolutely concrete solid. Maybe the "test" wasn't their test at all. Consider this thought: the test may have belonged to King Nebuchadnezzar and his men. Perhaps God used these three Jewish men to show himself to others. God has every right to use any one of us in order to reveal Himself to those who are watching our lives. We must be totally sold out to God. He owns our triumphs and our trials. We have given Him all rights to our lives to do as He pleases. So if He decides to put us in a furnace it may well be to strengthen our own faith or teach us an important life-changing lesson. However, it may also be that someone is watching and will take notice of who accompanies a Christian in the furnace. Always remember the impact of the scene that the king and his men were watching:

> Then king Nebuchadnezzar leaped to his feet in *amazement* and asked his advisers, "Weren't there three men that we tied up and threw into the fire?"
> They replied, "Certainly O king."
> He said, "*Look!* I see four... and the fourth looks like a son of the gods" (Dan. 3:24-25, *italics* added).

People are watching your life when you are in the fire. Who will they see beside you?

Throughout my nursing career, I have met many families and patients of faith. Many have openly shared their stories of pain, suffering, loss, or miracles. Regardless of the outcome of their stories, so many conclude with a question that baffles their minds, "How do people survive situations like mine without God?"

It is time for a piece of hurtful truth. There are people who live in this world without faith. They have no hope of heaven. No connection with God whatsoever. They never whisper His name nor feel His presence. Can we possibly imagine how devastating the furnace is for them? They, too, can be bound and thrown into the flames. This awareness affects me deeply. It quickly changes my self-absorbed question of "Lord, why me?" into this sincere statement of illumination, *"Better me, Lord, than someone without you."*

The desire of my heart is to live my life abiding by "The Whatever Principle" that the three men presented. It is their response that I chose to adopt in my life. Here is a paraphrase of their stance:

> I know that my God is *able* to *save* me from anything
> But even if He doesn't
> I will never doubt His love for me.
> I will continue to believe in Him.
> I will refuse to forsake Him.
> I will rely on His plan.

I will place my life in His capable hands and await His purpose for this situation and any other fire that appears in my life.

The greatest coping mechanism we can adopt is here before us. Loss and pain will appear over and over again at various points on the timeline of each of our lives. We must profess to the greatness and ability of God. He is able to save us from any situation, circumstance, or problem person in our life. No matter what we are facing, we must hold fast to the truth that our Father knows best. We may desperately desire rescue from a tragic situation, but if He chooses not to show up or intervene quickly, we must believe without a doubt that He will accomplish so much more by His divine decision to delay.

"The Whatever Principle" is clearly a way of life that is characterized by total surrender of our lives into the hands of God. We have seen this principle in action more than once by watching the life of Jesus.

In John 12: 27-28 Jesus is speaking: "Now my heart is troubled, and what shall I say? Father, save me from this hour? *No*, it was for this very reason I came to this hour. Father, glorify your name!" Then a voice came from heaven, "I have glorified it, and will glorify it again" (*italics* added).

Jesus withdrew from the disciples a little ways and knelt down and prayed, saying "Father, if you are willing, take this cup from me: Yet not my will but yours, be done" (Luke 22: 41-42).

Whatever, Father, whatever You decide. Whatever You want to accomplish with this life is entirely up to You. My life is Yours to do whatever You choose. By giving God and His will and choices precedence over our own comfort and our own desires, then we are living by "The Whatever Principle." Not my will, but God's will. It is never about us: it is always about God and His glorification.

Firmly believe that God is able to save you from anything... but even if He doesn't... accept whatever and anticipate the magnificent glory of God!

7. God's Gear

I HAVE THE PLEASURE OF working side by side with a devoted RN who is also a captain in the Army Reserves. She has prepared for war, trained in the trenches, fired weapons, and dressed out in the ultimate protective gear. One day I inquired if there was a specific name given for the garb used to deflect bullets and protect the body. Captain Duncan explained that the words "body armor" are the words used to describe the military gear intended to shield a person from injury and death.

God uses the very same terminology when He discusses the subject of protective gear for those enlisted in His service. The Lord talks about this subject in Ephesians 6 and repeatedly tells us to put on the full armor of God. I believe that God is saying that the only armor that is truly effective is the complete and careful coverage of our lives with God's design of security. His guaranteed power to withstand the enemy relies upon our knowledge and application of safety measures and combat essentials that He places in our hands. In the event that a section of our God-gear is missing, mishandled, or misunderstood, that body area is vulnerable to pain and severe injury from the enemy's attacks. The full body armor is needed and only the daily preparation and utilization of divine strategies and maneuvers will result in our ability to overcome and win the battles that we will face.

> Finally, be strong in the Lord and in his mighty power. Put on the full armor of God so that you can take your stand against the devil's schemes. For our struggle is not against flesh and blood, but against the rulers, against the authorities, against the powers of this dark world and against the spiritual forces of evil in the heavenly realms. Therefore put on the full armor of God, so that when the day of evil comes, you may be able to stand your ground, and after you have done everything, to stand. Stand firm then, with the belt of truth buckled around your waist, with the breastplate of righteousness in place, and with your feet fitted with the readiness that comes from the gospel of peace. In addition to all this, take up the shield of faith, with which you can extinguish all the flaming arrows of the evil one. Take the helmet of salvation and the sword of the Spirit, which is the word of God. And pray in the Spirit on all occasions with all kinds of prayers and requests. With this in mind, be alert and always keep on praying for all the saints (Eph. 6:10-18).

God, our commander and chief, has given us a lot of valuable information in those passages. It seems as though the day of evil is expected to come to us. God has made it clear that our struggle is not primarily physical in nature, but is definitely against spiritual forces of evil. God admonishes us over and over again to stand firm and be strong. His initial statement screams out the basis for our success. We are to be strong in the mighty power of the Lord. We cannot combat evil with our own strength and limited resources. It is when we acknowledge the strength and awesome tactics of our Lord that we can proceed. Consider this thought: participation in God's army begins with our *total surrender.*

Our primary objective is to stand our ground and curtail the devil's schemes. We must live our lives with the belt of truth secure around our waist. When we consider the purpose of a belt, a lot of different thoughts can fly around in our heads. A belt can keep a person's pants from falling down and causing an embarrassing moment. A belt can keep a blouse tucked neatly beneath a skirt. A sturdy belt can enable a person to easily reach frequently needed tools, such as a phone, flashlight, or beeper. A belt is centrally located and has a variety of functions. Essentially, when we think of Truth as a belt, we know that truth prevents embarrassing moments, and should be the center of a Christian life to holds things in place and make our words and actions dependable. Truth rings out and provides light and makes us available to others who may call or beep us for a response of integrity.

The breastplate of righteousness reminds me of the heart pillow that our patients receive after they undergo open-heart surgery. That incision requires protection, and the heart pillow is a wonderful reminder to hold onto and prevent injury. It also provides great support for the patients as they deep breathe and cough, which is a necessary evil in the post-operative period. In a similar way, righteousness also protects the heart.

The use of a few familiar colors can help us understand the actual definition of righteousness.

Today our society has a hard time dealing with the colors black and white. Gray seems to be the most prevalent shade that people prefer. When my son was a baby, his father would come home and sit in a black chair and hold little William. He would get so very upset that William would not look him in the eye. It wasn't until I explained the concept of an infant's visual capacity that he understood the reason for William's preferred gaze. Tiny ones have a limited clear vision and are attracted to contrasting colors. William wasn't looking into his father's face but was looking at his shoulder and intensely studying the contrast between his daddy's white shirt and the black leather chair.

It is such a shame that grown men and women refuse to study the contrast between black and white or right and wrong. There truly is a striking line of distinction. However, most have a tendency not to see the differences or choose to pretend that the lines of separation do not exist. The gray areas of tolerance, diminished sensitivity, and extreme indifference will never deflect attacks from the enemy. When the breastplate of righteousness is not in place, there is great danger of a heart attack that can be fatal.

First John 3:7 states it simply and to the point: "Dear children, do not let anyone lead you astray. He who does what is right is righteous, just as he is righteous." Protect yourself by knowing what is right, doing what is right, and protecting what is right in the eyes of God.

The thought of fitting our feet with the readiness that comes from knowing the gospel of peace gives new meaning to the variety of name brand shoes I have worn in my life. Nurses are on their feet the majority of time they are at work. I probably go through more shoes than most. I have narrow feet, and I have to wear good supportive shoes for I also have osteoarthritis in my knees. Through the years I have worn various types of power walkers from a variety of shoe manufacturers. Christians should be *Power Walkers* who carry the peace of the Gospel wherever they go. Are we fit with readiness, and do we embrace the gospel of peace? First Peter 3:15 addresses this very subject: "But in your hearts set apart Christ as Lord. Always be prepared to give an answer to everyone who asks you to give the reason for the hope that you have. But do this with gentleness and respect."

Once I attended a wonderful Christian candlelight service where many precious people with love in their eyes and hearts walked through a campground chapel singing songs of praise. As they passed by I had the strangest thought about a person walking down the hallway of a prison on the way to be executed. A guard announces, "Dead man walking." What a severe contrast to see such a display of Christian love expressed in all these people, I was seeing the "Holy Spirit walking." That is the One who needs to be in our *Easy Spirit* shoes giving us *New Balance* so that we can share God's peace. I know that this portion of God's holy armor is necessary for our protection, but I must share with you another purpose for this piece of power. I believe that this piece of armor aides us in enlisting men, as you will see by one of the most precious stories of my life.

I was working in the coronary care unit, and I had cared for a Mr. R. for several days. One morning he asked me, "Donna, why are you always so happy?"

I responded, "Well, do you want an answer, or do you want the truth?"

With a very serious tone he said, "I'd prefer the truth."

Looking into his eyes, I smiled and told him, "I believe that God loves me so much and it is that *knowing* that makes me very happy." We talked about what it meant to be a Christian. The gospel of peace is definitely a topic of interest when others notice a difference in attitude and behavior.

As He so often does, my "Paul Harvey God" let me know what happened to dear Mr. R. A year later, I transferred to the day surgery unit. My first day on the job, one of my patients was talking with a friend about Mr. R. They knew him well. They talked about him having a heart attack and being in the hospital. I told these women that I had the privilege of taking care of him. Then one of the women exclaimed, "You wouldn't believe what happened to him when he got home from the hospital after his heart attack. Why, he became a born-again Christian. Can you believe that?"

Are your feet fitted with readiness and your heart eager to exhibit the gospel of God's peace, not only for your own protection, but also for the intended purpose of enlisting others into the army of God?

Faith. God wants us to take up the shield of faith so that we can extinguish flaming arrows. Ask a Christian what exactly faith is, and they will quote Hebrews 11: 1: "Now faith is being sure of what we hope for and certain of what we do not see."

Ask a Christian who has been in church for years to paraphrase the definition of faith for a person who has never held a Bible, let alone ever heard of a chapter called Hebrews, and words fail them. As Christians we are familiar with the people and the stories that we find in this faith chapter:

> By faith we understand that the universe was formed at God's command, so that what is seen was not made out of what was visible. By faith Abel offered God a better sacrifice than Cain did. By faith he was commended as a righteous man, when God spoke well of his offerings. And by faith he still speaks, even though he is dead.
>
> By faith Enoch was taken from this life, so that he did not experience death; he could not be found, because God had taken him away. For before he was taken, he was commended

as one who pleased God. And without faith it is impossible to please God, because anyone who comes to him must believe that he exists and that he rewards those who earnestly seek him.

By faith Noah when warned about things not yet seen, in holy fear built an ark to save his family. By his faith he condemned the world and became heir of the righteousness that comes by faith.

By faith Abraham, when called to go to a place he would later receive as his inheritance, obeyed and went, even though he did not know where he was going. By faith he made his home in the Promised Land like a stranger in a foreign country; he lived in tents, as did Isaac and Jacob who were heirs with him of the same promise. For he was looking forward to the city with foundations, whose architect and builder is God (Heb. 11:3-8).

The chapter goes on and on, and the examples are more than this author can pen. How can we take the truth of these stories and find a way to explain the very essence of our Christian choice? How can we make the definition of faith understandable for all? I believe we must share current stories as well as the rich stories of our holy Scripture.

Faith is belief in God applied to life. Faith involves human action. It seems that faith consistently contains an element of the unknown. Faith is knowing God will get us where we need to go and the fact that we don't know where we are, simply doesn't matter. Faith is heeding God's words in the face of ridicule. It is Noah building a boat when there is no rain. It is a woman with a blood disease in the frenzy of a crowd, reaching out to touch a hem. It is a Nazarite with his hands on temple pillars open and available to the power of God. Faith is seen in the life of Donny.

I once had the unique pleasure of taking care of a very young man who had terrible heart disease and experienced an extremely long and complicated open-heart surgery. After surgery there was a rare complication. The physicians were not sure of the cause of the problem. One felt that the problem might have been caused by the length of time on the heart-lung machine. One felt it may have occurred due to a hypoxic event, or a period of time when the man's blood pressure dropped and oxygen was not available. Another thought it could be a blood clot shower that occluded vital arteries. Regardless of the cause, sweet Donny was blind. In all the years of my nursing career, I have never had to care for a "fresh" blind man. I cannot tell you how hard this was for me and how thankful I was that he could not see my tears. He was so kind and so appreciative of every thing I ever did for him.

Recovering well for any patient with heart surgery requires moving. Sitting in a chair for every meal and walking in the hall are essential to getting back to the routines of life. Donny would let us help him get up in the chair, but he continually refused to walk in the hall. One day I was helping him with his lunch and I asked him why he wouldn't walk with me. He became silent.

"Donny, are you afraid that you are going to fall?" I asked him.

He quietly answered, "Yes".

So, I proceeded to tell him about one of the favorite people in my life. Yolanda. She is one of the dearest women I have ever had the privilege to know and work beside. She has an uncanny way with patients. She is not a tiny lady, and I creatively told Donny that she was strong and would never let him fall. Truthfully, I told him that my grandmother wore a size 44 bra and I thought she was buxom, but Yo definitely had Grandma beat! When Donny smiled and even laughed a little, I knew that I had succeeded in giving him an accurate mental picture of my friend. So I asked him, if Yolanda and I would help him in the hall, would he please walk with us? I promised him that we would never let him fall and that we would only go as far as he felt that he could. We would be right beside him. He agreed. I found Yo.

To see my friend interact with Donny was such a joy. She connected with him right away and guided him with her words of encouragement. He did everything that he could to please her and followed her instructions to a "T" while building confidence with each move. Yolanda and I, and a terrified blind man, who was totally dependent on our voices, our directions, and our presence, walked that hall together.

I honestly don't know of a more precious image of true faith than the one Yolanda and Donny have given me. Do you see faith? Faith is total dependence on God's voice, His direction and His presence as we walk the halls of life together.

One Thanksgiving my father-in-law helped me to understand the helmet of salvation. My husband's family gathered in the living room after eating dinner. We began to talk with Pops about the war. He had driven a tank in WWII and was telling us some of the situations he had lived through. During the conversation, he told us that the helmets they wore while inside the tanks were never meant to deflect bullets; they were intended to prevent minor head injuries when the terrain was rough and the guys were knocked around inside the tanks. Infantry had a different kind of helmet made out of a bullet-resistant material that provided those men with a greater amount of protection because their risk of being shot in the head was greater than the risk of the men inside the tanks.

When our God talks about our helmet of salvation, I believe that the purpose of the helmet is to provide a barrier from negative, hopeless thoughts. If the reality of salvation is in our mind, we cannot fear death or any other circumstance, for daily we should enjoy the knowledge that we are already living eternal life. Our thoughts must be guarded and our minds must concentrate on the words of our God. We can think about the power of what Christ is able to continually do for us. Hebrews 7:25 promises, "Therefore he is able to save completely those who come to God through him, because he always lives to intercede for them."

Hebrews 13:6 provides us with another marvelous concept: "So we say with confidence, "The Lord is my helper; I will not be afraid. What can man do to me?"

Wear the helmet of salvation and protect your mind. You have been completely, not partially, saved through Christ. He always intercedes for you. Keep those thoughts in the forefront of your mind, and there will be no room for fear. Have confidence in your Commander.

The sword of the Spirit is the Word of God; there is not a subject that is not addressed in the Bible. There is an answer for all the questions in life. God is eloquent and consistent in His instructions and commands. Each of us must desire to acquire these principles and apply them to our lives as naturally and effortlessly as we breathe. The living word of God should be expressed, daily, through the lives of those who claim Him.

Know His Word, love His Word, live His Word; as you protect your own life, you protect His resource.

Protection requires prayer for anything, at anytime, and for you or anyone else. My brother and his wife have friends who have experienced a great deal of personal tragedy. Their son got one of his dad's guns and shot and killed his friend. Because the boy had loaded the empty gun prior to it going off, he was held as an adult until the authorities could determine if the shooting was intentional versus accidental. He went to jail and while there, became drug addicted. It was a devastating time for this family; however, they became Christians. The son suffered from addiction, even though the shooting was finally declared accidental and he was freed. Years passed. One night this same young man was killed in a car accident. One of the most important points that this father spoke to me about was prayer. He said that there were times when he could not pray. He felt such a distance. It was as if his prayers could not rise above the ceiling.

In the event that there are ever times in your life when you experience what seems to be a deafening silence from God, this man wants you to know that, "That's okay. When you can't pray, others' prayers will cover you. When the distance seems immense and the silence seems unbearable, remember that your brothers and sisters in Christ are holding you up, conveying your heart and needs when you can't get a word out. Someone is whispering your name into the ear of God when you haven't got the energy to speak one word."

Is it any wonder that part of our protection is prayer for all the saints? Perhaps our prayers build hedgerows, unify the troops, and provide access to the most powerful weapon available. Prayer gives us audience with the Commander, and we can reason together, consider possibilities together and obtain specific personal edicts. Consider this question, "Can Satan hear our prayers?" I don't believe he can. So when we pray, I believe that we not only have the heart and attention of our Lord, but we have a private line. Prayer is sacred, secret, personal, intimate, powerful communication with the God who wants us alive, protected, and living our lives as He leads and directs. Christians need to be clothed in the full armor that only He can provide for us. Captain Duncan says that the best dress uniform is called "Class A." God's gear is full body armor, and we are dressed out whenever we have each piece properly in place, and then we are ready for action. Our next step lies in identification of the enemy and his tactics.

8. Enemy Tactics

HE WAS THE MODEL OF PERFECTION, full of wisdom, and perfect in beauty. He was in Eden, the garden of God; every precious stone adorned him: ruby, topaz and emerald, chrysolite, onyx and jasper, sapphire, turquoise and beryl. His settings and mountings were made of gold: on the day he was created they were prepared. He was anointed as a guardian cherub, for God ordained him. He was on the Holy Mount of God: He walked among the fiery stones. He was blameless in his ways from the day he was created until the day that he sinned (paraphrase of Ezekiel 28: 12-15).

The story of Lucifer, the guardian cherub, one of God's splendid creations became arrogant, prideful, filled with violence, wickedness, and self-adoration. Lucifer was created to give glory and honor and praise to God with the heavenly faithful. This angel did not appreciate his position nor accept the purpose of his being. In Isaiah 14:3, the prophet reveals his personal objective:

"You said in your heart, 'I will ascend to heaven; I will raise my throne above the stars of God; I will set enthroned on the mount of assembly, on the utmost heights of the sacred mountain. I will ascend above the tops of the clouds; I will make myself like the Most High.'"

Satan, Lucifer, the morning star, Beelzebub, prince of this world—regardless which of his names is used—has one primary motive and it will always be the same. He is determined to dethrone God and run the world, for he believes he never was created to be anything less than God. He is the author of "me-ism" and the true example of covetousness. Ruling the universe is a job that does not belong to him, yet he lusts after it. Sitting on a throne and being like God is not a goal incorporated into his original job description, yet he has taken the liberty to rewrite his own plans, goals, and objectives. He chucked God's original design for his existence, and his modifications resulted in the disgust of God. So God proceeded to chuck Satan and his followers out of His heaven. There are a multitude of verbs used for Lucifer's departure as found in Scripture:

> "Through your widespread trade you were filled with violence and you sinned. So *I drove you* in disgrace from the mount of God, and *I expelled you*, O guardian cherub, from among the fiery stones. Your heart became proud on account of your beauty and you corrupted your wisdom because of your splendor. So *I threw you to the earth*;
> I made a spectacle of you before kings. By your many sins and dishonest trade you have desecrated your sanctuaries . . ." (Ezek. 28:16-18, *italics* added).

> "How you have fallen from heaven, O morning star, son of the dawn!
> You have been *cast down* to earth, you who once laid low the nations! (Isa. 14:12, *italics* added).

"Chucked" isn't found in the Scriptures, but it seems to fit in nicely with the other verbs found in our text: drove, expelled, threw, and cast. Revelation 12:4 also lets us know that Satan didn't leave alone. "His tail swept a third of the stars out of the sky and flung them to earth." Even in Matthew 25:41, Jesus in a story makes this statement, "Depart from me, you who are cursed, into the eternal fire prepared for the devil and his angels."

So the devil is real, and he has an army of evil combatants at his disposal. He is motivated by his pure hatred of God and his unquenchable desire to acquire all the things that belong to God. Do you understand the gravity of this truth? If you belong to God the devil wants you, and he will work incessantly to wear you down, to break your spirit, destroy your witness, and make you unrighteous. He wants you to doubt your faith; he savors captivating your mind and distracting you from time with God in prayer or Bible study. He loves to find a way to give you lead feet so that you refrain from action and never take the first step to share God's gospel.

God's plan of salvation for all mankind abolished sin and death through the sacrifice and resurrection of Jesus Christ. It is vital to understand that the central focus of God's enemy is to negate the power of the cross, provide a banquet table of succulent sin for all mankind to consume at will, and utilize numerous tactics to prevent or damage God's plans in any way possible. These very tactics must be considered and revealed. Anyone who is involved in the armed services is aware of the importance of gathering intelligence. Vital information includes the following:

- what we know about us
- what we know about the enemy
- what we think the enemy knows about us

This process exposes both our strengths and vulnerabilities, therefore helping us to efficiently secure our defenses and keep our perimeters intact and insurmountable. We must be willing to dispose of our blinders and naïve perceptions.

Satan and his angels survived the fall to earth. They are hard at work. In this chapter, we must explore areas of Scripture that can make some people uneasy and frightened. Yet I believe that revealing the enemy's tactics can only heighten our awareness, strengthen our resolve, and quicken our responses. The desired outcome of this chapter is to expose the tactics repeatedly utilized by God's enemy. Understanding the potential damage that can occur in our lives is of utmost importance, for oftentimes Satan's attacks and successes are due to people's ignorance, improper attire, and more than likely inconsistency. We have discussed the importance of the protective gear that God has purposely designed for all who are on active duty or for any who are willing to enlist. Absence of any piece of God's gear can result in vulnerability, breach of security, and potential risk to life. As we embark on our military endeavors it is essential for all to recognize upfront that Satan's tactics are nothing but lies and his plan of action is to entice people to embrace his lies as innocent, acceptable, and justified life choices.

Enemy Tactic 1: "There is no such place as hell! The devil does not exist! There will never be a judgment day!"

One of the quickest, least time-consuming devices that the devil enjoys to see in action is Tactic 1: he loves people to deny his existence or that there is such a place as hell. He is so relieved when people make comments such as:

"If God is a loving God, why would there be a hell? There can't be a hell or a devil. For God came to save us not punish us."

"How can there be a hell after death? My life on earth is hell. If there is a hell, I've already served my time."

"Only stupid people would ever believe that the devil or demons actually exist."

"Everyone goes to heaven when they die. God is love and He loves us all."

Now aren't those pleasant, fluffy thoughts? Believing in this tactic simply erases any source of evil as well as any punishment and exempts humans from receiving an evaluation of their life from God. When people choose to believe that there is no hell or punishment for evil, they are adopting a very dangerous theory of the enemy. If we examine God's holy Word, we cannot find justification for this lie. Satan is discussed, and so is hell. Jesus Christ spoke of both, and what He said isn't "fluffy and sweet." In Luke 16:19-31, Christ gave us a description of hell in a parable that contains the devastation and despair of a man who was once a very wealthy individual.

"There was a rich man who was dressed in purple and fine linen and lived in luxury every day. At his gate was laid a beggar

named Lazarus, covered with sores and longing to eat what
fell from the rich man's table. Even the dogs came and licked
his sores.

"The time came when the beggar died and the angels carried him to Abraham's side. The rich man also died and was
buried. In hell, where he was in torment, he looked up and
saw Abraham far away, with Lazarus by his side. So he called
to him, 'Father Abraham, have pity on me and send Lazarus
to dip the tip of his finger in water and cool my tongue,
because I am in agony in this fire.'

"But Abraham replied, 'Son, remember that in your lifetime you received your good things while Lazarus received
bad things, but now he is comforted here and you are in
agony. And besides all this, between us and you a great chasm
has been fixed, so that those who want to go from here to you
cannot, nor can anyone cross over from there to us.'

"He answered, 'Then I beg you, father, send Lazarus to my
father's house, for I have five brothers. Let him warn them, so
that they will not also come to this place of torment.'

"Abraham replied, 'They have Moses and the Prophets; let
them listen to them.' 'No, father Abraham,' he said, 'but if
someone from the dead goes to them, they will repent.'

"He said to him, 'If they do not listen to Moses and the
Prophets, they will not be convinced even if someone rises
from the dead'" (Luke 16:19-31).

No hell? I don't believe that Jesus would ever paint such a graphic
picture of a place of torment and agony if it were not so. But deny or
ignore that such a place exists and you many wind up there, just as this
rich man did. That outcome would sure please the devil.

Essentially, Satan's primary motivation is to take as many of us as he
possibly can into the very depths of hell. If you have difficulty believing in the devil and his motives, let us examine the heart of Christ as he
portrayed Satan's methods.

Jesus told them another parable:

"The kingdom of heaven is like a man who sowed good
seed in his field. But while everyone was sleeping, his enemy

came and sowed weeds among the wheat, and went away. When the wheat sprouted and formed heads, then the weeds also appeared.

"The owner's servants came to him and said, 'Sir, didn't you sow good seed in your field? Where then did the weeds come from?'"

"'An *enemy* did this,' he replied.

"The servants asked him, 'Do you want us to go and pull them up?'"

"'No,' he answered, 'because while you are pulling the weeds, you may root up the wheat with them. Let both grow together until the harvest. At that time I will tell the harvesters: First collect the weeds and tie them in bundles to be burned; then gather the wheat and bring it into my barn'" (Matt. 13:24-30).

In Matthew 13: 37-43, Jesus then explained this parable to his disciples.

He answered, "The one who sowed the good seed is the Son of Man. The field is the world, and the good seed stands for the sons of the kingdom. The weeds are the sons of the evil one, and *the enemy is the devil*. The harvest is the end of the age, and the harvesters are angels.

"As the weeds are pulled up and burned in the fire, so it will be at the end of the age. The Son of Man will send out his angels, and they will weed out of his kingdom everything that causes sin and all who do evil. They will throw them into the fiery furnace where there will be weeping and gnashing of teeth. Then the righteous will shine like the sun in the kingdom of their Father. He who has ears, let him hear" (*italics* added).

In this passage Jesus clearly identified the evil one as the devil, and He also spoke of those who follow Satan as the sons of the evil one. Their end will not be pretty. They will not be rejoicing in the presence of God, but will be in continual torment. Is God the God of love and forgiveness? The answer to that question is "absolutely." However, a twisted truth or a half-truth does not equal *truth*. The truth about God concerning his hearts desire in the salvation of humankind is revealed in 2 Peter 3: 9. This scripture tells us that God wishes that no one would perish and that all would come to eternal life through repentance. God came that you might have life and have it more abundantly. The devil prefers that you die in your sins, and spend eternity in hell. His plan is so opposite of God's. Think about this, God requires that you believe and confess with your mouth and heart that Jesus is Lord. Deny that Satan exists and live a life with the objective of self-indulgence, pleasure, and blatant sin, and you have met the requirements of eternal separation from a God who has loved you since you were conceived.

Denial is a marvelous mechanism that enables people to cloud the issues and blur reality. When people deny evil, Satan, and the existence of hell, they are essentially denying that there will be a Judgment Day. If one truly believes that actions and behaviors are never going to be evaluated by a higher authority than man, there is no restraint available for evil. Nor is there any fear of eternal punishment even though Revelation 20:11-15 discusses Judgment and the books that document the legacy of our lives and eternal destiny:

> Then I saw a great white throne and him who was seated on it. Earth and sky fled from his presence, and there was no place for them. And I saw the dead, great and small, standing before the throne, and books were opened. Another book was opened, which is the book of life. The dead were judged according to what they had done as recorded in the books. The sea gave up the dead that were in it and death and Hades gave up the dead that were in them and *each person was judged according to what he had done*. Then death and Hades were thrown into the lake of fire. The lake of fire is the second death. If anyone's name was not found written in the book of life, he was thrown into the lake of fire (*italics* added).

When people live as though Satan isn't real, there is no fear of his interventions, temptations, or attacks. When a person lives a life thinking Satan is a mythical creature, that person will never prepare, or protect himself or herself or anyone they love. Your life and your family are not prepared, and that lack of protection leaves all that you love standing defenseless and ignorant in a wide, open field. He can strike you down and you'll never know what hit you.

Heads up! He's real! He's nasty, and you had best wake up and be on alert. Eternity awaits us all, and in this life we are all involved in a spiritual battle. Don't you want all of your loved ones' names written in the Lamb's Book of Life? Don't you want to participate in the holy army of God? Stop denying the existence of Satan, and take the time to study God's plan of action for this life and the next. Denial leads to death—eternal death. That's a long time to spend away from God. If you believe in Christ and what He says, you cannot deny Satan, hell or the promise of justice from a Holy God.

When we go into an ice cream shop, we get to choose whatever we want. We can have a milkshake, sherbet, or a sundae with a variety of toppings. We can order an ice cream cone or have a couple different flavors in a waffle cone or a sugar cone. We can even order ice cream in a cup and eat it with a plastic spoon. We can pick and choose whatever we want. That works for an ice cream shop.

Christianity was never meant to be a "pick and choose what you want" religion. We cannot wander through the Bible and choose what we will believe and what we won't. We cannot choose God's love, heaven, forgiveness, peace, joy, and all of the sweetness Christ offers and ignore the fact that there are some very unpleasant, distasteful elements in our world that will result in the wrath of God.

I believe that it is a very dangerous area for anyone to claim Christ and deny Satan. I firmly believe the total package of Christianity includes the absolute trust and credibility of every word of Jesus Christ. Christ never denied Satan, and we shouldn't either. Christ endured being tempted by Satan. Christ rebuked him. Christ acknowledged his existence and foretold his demise. If you know Christ, you know that His enemy exists. If you know Scripture, you know Satan exists, hell is a real place, and judgment of evil is a promise, so don't fall for enemy Tactic 1.

Enemy Tactic 2: The Ladder of Rationalization

Have you ever imagined that rationalization can be a tool that Satan can use to escalate a person up the ladder of evil intentions one rung at a time? When a person develops justification for unkind behaviors and actions, each wicked deed diminishes conviction and instead brings alongside a portion of tolerance, arrogance, and pride. Satan can use rationalization and excuses on anyone who will listen to his voice and act according to his guidance. He can persuade and nudge people into dangerous areas of sinful activity. He can use Christians and non-Christians. His pattern is to accentuate a person's natural bent and escalate them step-by-step to higher degrees of cruel or evil behavior through the tactic of self-righteous rationalization.

Suppose a woman is a terrible gossip. She is your co-worker, and you can be sure that her conversation is, as always, judgmental and critical of everything and everyone from the janitor to the president of the institution. She never has a kind thing to say about anyone at anytime. Her tongue is her instrument, and under Satan's guidance she uses this tool to hurt, break down, discredit and harm other people. She may appear to be kind and helpful to some, yet behind their backs she delights in malicious gossip and character assassination.

One morning her tongue gets out of control, and she threatens to shoot a co-worker in the privacy of a locked office. Satan moves her up a step on the ladder of evil ways. Once this behavior is reported, she makes the decision to lie. She rationalizes that she cannot risk telling the truth; she might lose her job. She denies that she ever threatened her co-worker. Satan smiles as this woman quickly becomes comfortable justifying her lie.

The deceitful progression gets easier. Now to give credence to her major lie, she reasons that she must fabricate a plausible story, painting the woman that reported the threat as a hateful person, who for no reason made up this horrible tale. Satan begins her training on how to devise a wicked scheme and falsely accuse an innocent person of lying. Satan must be rolling in laughter to see *his liar* so eagerly falsely accuse a truthful person. This woman has experienced no conviction of wrong-doing. She has totally rationalized her evil ways as justification to keep her job and as she becomes more and more comfortable in her walk with the devil, she begins to boast and brag. She sways her friends to believe her sad situation of such unjust treatment. She becomes proud, belligerent, and defiant in spirit. Look at her success story closely:

One who once was a gossip became…
one who threatened another with bodily harm.
Then she became a woman who devised a wicked scheme.
With ease she took on the position of false witness of an innocent person.
Then she developed a haughty, prideful, boasting spirit.

Is she a successful woman? In the eyes of evil, absolutely! How about in your eyes? Have you ever had the misfortune to know such a person? Maybe you are that person. Maybe you are the one who has received the threat. Maybe you believe the liar. Maybe you are a friend of the one threatened. Maybe you don't know who or what to believe, but you hate the whole scenario. If you wonder why, I can tell you: God hates it too. Have you ever considered that there are things that God hates?

Proverbs 6:16-19 tells us exactly how successful this woman is in the eyes of God.

> "There are six things the Lord hates, seven that are detestable to him:
> Haughty Eyes
> A Lying Tongue
> Hands that Shed Innocent Blood
> A Heart the Devises Wicked Schemes
> Feet that are Quick to Rush into Evil
> A False Witness Who Pours Out Lies
> A Man Who Stirs Up Dissension Among Brothers."

Satan can persuade anyone to use rationalization to cause pain and destroy the peace of others. Satan can help Christians up the same ladder of evil ways, and people of God can climb quite high. There is a story of a king who also climbed that ladder, while Satan attempted to destroy a man after God's own heart.

Second Samuel chapters 11and 12 tells the story of a king appointed by God who saw a beautiful woman bathing: another man's wife; a woman the king wanted even though she did not belong to him. He inquired about her and was told that she was the wife of Uriah, a man who was a military officer in the king's service. Regardless of this knowledge, the king summoned her to his palace. This man and woman willingly committed adultery. She was married, and so was King David. The woman, Bathsheba became pregnant. What a mess.

Now the king had to devise a scheme. He tried to find a deceitful way to cover up his sin. He rationalized that if Uriah could have sex with Bathsheba, he would think that the baby conceived was his own. The king would be off the hook, and no one would know what had happened behind a closed, locked door.

So King David called Uriah to the palace and met him face-to-face. Under the pretence of discussing the events of the war, he spent time with Uriah. He then sent him home along with a gift. What a genuine act of kindness!

Sadly for the king, Uriah was an upright man, and he refused to enjoy the arms of his wife when his men were camped in open fields, so he slept at the entrance of the palace. David pressed Uriah to stay another night and even tried to get him drunk so that his moral fabric would weaken, and he would go home and sleep with his wife. Uriah was a greater man than the king for he was a man of resolve and self-control. He did not go home. So the next morning David's feet sped quickly to rush into a higher level of evil. Climbing higher, nearing the top rung of a very unstable ladder, David had Uriah put into the front line of the fiercest point of battle.

He may have rationalized his action with this thought, *War kills. No one will question Uriah's death. I am home free.*

Thus David gave instructions to Joab: "Put Uriah in the front line where the fighting is fiercest. Then withdraw from him so he will be struck down and die" (2 Samuel 11:14-15).

Joab obeyed the King and sent back the message, "mission accomplished."

David's response to Joab was so cold. "Don't let this upset you; the sword devours one as well as another . . ."(2 Sam. 22:25).

He simply was telling Joab exactly what he was telling himself. He felt self-absolved and guiltless. David sinned and got away with it, or did he?

"After the time of mourning was over, David had Bathsheba brought to his house, and she soon became his wife and bore him a son. *The thing David had done displeased the Lord*" (2 Sam. 11:27, *italics* added).

Proverbs 21:30 assures, "There is no wisdom, no insight, no plan that can succeed against the Lord."

Not even King David's scheme could slip by unnoticed by God. In 2 Samuel 12, God sent Nathan the prophet to David and his sin was brought to light.

The Lord sent Nathan to David. When he came to him, he said, "There were two men in a certain town, one rich and the other poor. The rich man had a very large number of sheep and cattle, but the poor man had nothing except one little ewe lamb he had bought. He raised it, and it grew up with him and his children. It shared his food, drank from his cup and even slept in his arms. It was like a daughter to him.

"Now a traveler came to the rich man, but the rich man refrained from taking one of his own sheep or cattle to prepare a meal for the traveler who had come to him. Instead, he took the ewe lamb that belonged to the poor man and prepared it for the one who had come to him."

David burned with anger against the man and said to Nathan, "As surely as the Lord lives, the man who did this deserves to die! He must pay for that lamb four times over, because he did such a thing and had no pity."

Then Nathan said to David, *You are the man!*"

"This is what the Lord, the God of Israel, says:

"'I anointed you king over Israel, and I delivered you from the hand of Saul. I gave your master's house to you, and your master's wives into your arms. I gave you the house of Israel and Judah. And if all this had been too little, I would have given you even more. Why did you despise the word of the Lord by doing what is evil in his eyes? You struck down Uriah the Hittite with the sword and took his wife to be your own. You killed him with the sword of the Ammonites. Now, therefore, the sword will never depart from your house, because you despised me and took the wife of Uriah the Hittite to be your own'

"This is what the Lord says: 'Out of your own household I am going to bring calamity upon you. Before your very eyes I will take your wives and give them to one who is close to you, and he will lie with your wives in broad daylight. You did it in secret, but I will do this thing in broad daylight before all Israel'" (*italics* added).

Can you smell the aroma of Satan? Can you clearly see his pattern of rationalization? Participation in an activity that is unbecoming and distressing to the Lord. Wanting something or someone that does not belong to you and manipulating circumstances to obtain that thing or person regardless of the peripheral damage that occurs. Damage to innocent people is usually the result of the ladder of evil collapsing. Evil has consequences. The baby conceived in sin died.

When Satan instructs someone in his ways of deceitfulness and the use of rationalization, those who are on the receiving end of the lies, gossip, wicked schemes, or false accusation must take heart in knowing that God sees it all, and God will repay. He promises this in Romans 12:19, "Do not take revenge, my friends, but leave room for God's wrath, for it is written: It is mine to avenge: I will repay says the Lord."

When people believe that they have successfully protected themselves by a covering of lies, the sadness is that there will be a day when they will stand before the Almighty God and on that day, what was done in darkness will be exposed by God's examination light!

Nathan the prophet made it very clear how God interpreted King David's escalating evil. God took it personally, and He reminded David of all that He had given him in the past and informed him that He would have been happy to give him even more. Yet, David despised the word of the Lord and did what was evil in the sight of God. Satan can and does use this tactic to create havoc. He whispers evil ideas and rationalizations into the ears of anyone who will listen.

"No one will ever know. Go ahead take it. You deserve it."

"It's your body, and you can do whatever you want with it."

"You're not hurting anyone!"

"Who would ever believe that? No one will ever find out the truth."

"Go ahead and do it; everyone else does."

I had a cake made for a friend's birthday and took it to his workplace to celebrate. It was lovely. The frosting was beautiful, and the decorations and candles looked perfect. We took pictures, sang 'Happy

Birthday' and the man made a wish and blew out the candles. Then we all anxiously awaited a piece of cake. With our plates ready and our mouths watering, the birthday guy tried to cut a piece of cake, but his knife couldn't penetrate the cake. It was a frosted cardboard box. It wasn't what it appeared to be at all. It was made to look like something it wasn't. Of course the real cake was in the break-room. So what is the point?

No matter how Satan tries to decorate his underlying activity, it is always the same. He is a liar. No matter how you frost it, justify it, or try to rationalize it, lies are lies. There is no excuse or justification that can sugarcoat any lie. Lying is wrong, and it is Satan's passion. Each tactic Satan uses is a lie. His primary motivation is for people to believe his lies.

Enemy Tactic 3: Dream Labels of False Accusation

We have repeatedly emphasized this fact: the true mark of Satan is deceitful methodology. The mark of Christianity is honesty and truth. Christ Himself with intense emotion addressed this issue during an encounter with the Pharisees in John 8:42-47. In this passage He provides us with the extreme paradox between Himself (Truth) and Satan (liar).

> Jesus said to them, "If God were your Father you would love me, for I came from God and now am here. I have not come on my own: but he sent me. Why is my language not clear to you? Because you are unable to hear what I say. You belong to your father, the devil, and you want to carry out your father's desire. He was a murderer from the beginning, not holding to the truth, for there is no truth in him. When he lies, he speaks his native language, for he is a liar and the father of lies. Yet because I tell the truth, you do not believe me! Can any of you prove me guilty of sin? If I am telling the truth, why won't you believe me? He who belongs to God hears what God says. The reason you do not hear is that you do not belong to God."

These Jews proceeded to say terrible things to Christ. They accused Him of being demon-possessed. They asked Him in John 8:53, "Who do you think you are?"

Jesus replied: "If I glorify myself, my glory means nothing. My Father, whom you claim as your God, is the one who glorifies me. Though you do not know him, I know him. If I said I did not, I would be a liar just like you, but I know him and keep his word" (John 8: 53-54).

Jesus does not water down His observations of evil people nor does He ignore the source. He makes very clear, concise points. Notice that the Pharisees are deaf to the truth because of their intimate relationship with the devil. Christ does not apologize or try to soften the sting of His words. He openly identifies the liar. Some of us may read this and think that it is a bit harsh of the Lord to say, "I'm not a liar like you." I doubt that many of us would look someone square in the face and say, "You are a liar." However Christ can. He knows a liar when He sees one. When two accusers point fingers at one another, He knows the one who speaks truth and the one who lies. No truthful person ever is required to produce a defense before God, for God knows those who belong to Him.

In the scripture above, did you notice that the ability to hear the truth is connected to family ties? Those who are connected to the devil cannot hear the truth. They cannot even understand the language, let alone decipher meanings or intent. Those who belong to God believe Christ, and they can hear when God speaks. Notice also the same wicked device that Satan continually uses. The Pharisees accused Christ of being demon-possessed. It's ironic that Christ just finished identifying these people as children of the devil, and they quickly turned around and labeled Christ as "demon or devil-possessed." This is similar to the section titled *Enemy Tactic 2* where the gossip called an innocent woman a liar. Devil-driven people call Christ demon-possessed.

This tactic of Satan's is to label those in his opposition with the titles and accusations he can only dream that we would partake of! Satan would love to possess Christ. He would love for Christ to turn to him. In Matthew 4: 8, we see one of the dreams of Satan.

Again the devil took Him to a very high mountain and showed Him all the kingdoms of the world and their splendor. "All this I will give you," he said, "if you will bow down and worship me."

But Christ worships only his Father, and Satan can label Him, but the label doesn't change the allegiance of the Son. Satan would also love for innocent, committed Christians to cross over and become deceitful people. He would love it if Christians would do all the things that are disgusting in the eyes of God. Then we would begin to listen to the voice of the devil, and we would gradually change sides, abandon our families, and exchange fathers. How absolutely terrifying is that thought? Is it possible? Yes. Does it happen? Sadly, yes. It can happen to anyone at anytime. Devoted Christians or lost individuals can listen to God or listen to Satan. We need to be aware that this can happen in a moment. If it can happen to Peter, then I am sure it can happen to you or me.

In Matthew 16: 13-18 Jesus asked the disciples this question:

"Who do people say the Son of Man is?" They replied, "Some say John the Baptist, others say Elijah; and still others, Jeremiah or one of the prophets."

"But what about you?" he asked, "Who do you say that I am?"

Simon Peter answered, "You are the Christ, the Son of the living God."

Jesus replied, "Blessed are you Simon Son of Jonah, for this was not revealed to you by man, but by my Father in heaven. I tell you that you are Peter and on this rock will I build my church...."

This passage revealed Peter listening to God. In the same chapter, verses 21-23, we find Peter listening to a different voice.

From that time on Jesus began to explain to his disciples that he must go to Jerusalem and suffer many things at the hands of the elders, chief priests and teachers of the law, and that he must be killed and on the third day be raised to life.

Peter took him aside and began to rebuke him. "Never, Lord!" he said. "This shall never happen to you!"

Jesus turned and said to Peter, "Get behind me, Satan! You are a stumbling block to me; you do not have in mind the things of God, but the things of men."

Be careful to discern the voice you hear. Satan can be persuasive when he has your full attention. Remember that he can sway people into wicked schemes that are extremely painful and destructive. He can use false accusation to label people, and it is heartbreaking, especially if the label is applied by the lies of a family member or someone you have trusted and loved.

Just this past year, I met an 86-year-old blind woman, who shared her brother's tragedy with me as I walked her in the hall. Her brother, Bob had always loved his family, so he parceled his land and generously gave his children adjoining property in order to build their homes and raise their families all around him. One son needed money badly and devised a scheme with the hope of forcing his father to sell his homestead and all of his remaining property so that he could profit by an early inheritance.

The son accused his father of sexually abusing one of his granddaughters. The courts made Bob move into an apartment for they decided he was living too close to his alleged victim. However, the judge did not require him to liquidate his property nor to pay his son any damages.

This sad, old man is a widow. He can never see his children, nor can he ever spend time with the sweet grandbabies he loves so much. Several of his sisters believe the lies, but his dear blind sister encourages him and loves him dearly. Bob is devastated. It is a tragedy when your children want only your money and no relationship or love.

Scripture tells us in I Timothy 6:10, "For the love of money is the root of all kinds of evil. . . ."

This incident shows how false accusation and the label of a child sex offender is placed on a father by a son with greed as his sole motivation. We never want to imagine that such things happen, but they do. They happen more often that we realize.

Some cannot endure the mental anguish nor accept the dream label applied to their life. So is the story of Charlie.

Charlie's Choice

One evening the phone rang at Cindy and Larry's house. A man asked to speak to Larry.

"Hey Larry this is Charlie. I'm in trouble. Could you help me?"

"Sure Charlie, what's going' on?"

"I'm in jail at Salem. Could you come and bail me out? I need your help."

Charlie and his brother had lived in the same town for thirty years. They seldom spent time together nor did they talk often. But this night Larry jumped into his truck and made the two-hour trip to Salem in record time. He never imagined all that he would have to do in order to help his brother. Charlie had specific instructions and explained the stressful situation.

A woman he had loved years ago had come forward claiming he had sexually assaulted her young daughter who now was a teenager. There wasn't a shred of evidence—only her word against his.

Charlie had worked very hard all of his life and invested well. He had never married, and up front it was made known that if he would pay a hefty amount of money all the charges would be dropped without question, trial, or jail time.

A man accused.

At one of the hearings where the young teen testified on the stand, Larry and his wife were in the courtroom. From their seats they watched as she kept slyly giving her mother the 'thumbs-up' sign as she verbally destroyed Charlie's reputation.

With many detailed counts against him, prison was Charlie's certain destination. For seven months the clouds of despair and stress covered the lives of his family. Yet the relationship that developed between the two brothers was extremely tight. Larry and Cindy never once asked any questions of Charlie. Their home became a refuge for him. He would come every Thursday evening for supper. He was so overwhelmed by his brother and sister-in-law's unconditional love and help that he could never do enough for them. He showered them with elaborate gourmet foods. He would have given them anything he owned.

A man accused, falls into a despair and hopelessness that few of us could ever imagine.

One Thursday morning unexpectedly, he came to Cindy and Larry's and discussed the possible outcomes that would be made in court. They talked about the supper menu. But Charlie never showed up at the house that night. Instead a call came from the police. The groceries were still in his vehicle when Cindy and Larry arrived at Charlie's garage. He had laid his work gloves on the hood of the SUV, after he finished tying the rope that would choke the life out of his body. He was 65 years old and the thought of spending the rest of his life in prison was more than he could bear.

A man accused may be totally innocent, yet the accusations alone can destroy family ties and ruin lives. Some men cannot imagine life in prison labeled as a child molester. Family members may not be supportive, may refuse to discuss things and may be so ashamed they do not come near the accused. If accusation alone proved a man guilty of a crime, the legal system could save time and money. Just lock up all the accused and throw away the key. Sadly, not all people tell the truth.

When a person lies about the behavior and actions of another, that person is not only causing harm to the one they are attacking, but also unknowingly, they are damaging the very life that they possess. It is not a coincidence that God addresses liars in the Bible. God doesn't leave any room for debate when it comes to his feelings about those who lie, falsely accuse others, or take revenge on others.

Psalm 119: 69-71, 78 reads, "Though the arrogant have smeared me with lies, I keep your precepts with all my heart. Their hearts are callous and unfeeling but I delight in your law. It was good for me to be afflicted so that I might learn your decrees. May the arrogant be put to shame for wronging me without a cause, but I will meditate on your precepts."

So when you are afflicted, study God's precepts and find out what His thoughts and feelings are concerning your situation. Being on the receiving end of vicious behavior is never pleasant, but Scripture searches of the subject matter may open your heart to this startling truth: *your enemy is in a worse predicament than you will ever be.* The Lord addresses their promised outcome and His reaction to their wickedness in these scriptures.

A false witness will perish and whoever listens to him will be destroyed forever (Prov. 21:28).

I will set before my eyes no vile thing. The deeds of faithless men I hate; they will not cling to me. Men of perverse heart shall be far from me; I will have nothing to do with evil. Whoever slanders his neighbor in secret, him will I put to silence; whoever has haughty eyes and a proud heart, him will I not endure. My eyes will be on the faithful in the land, that they may dwell with me; he whose walk is blameless will minister to me. No one who practices deceit will dwell in my house; no one who speaks falsely will stand in my presence. Every morning I will put to silence all the wicked in the land; I will cut off every evildoer from the city of the Lord (Ps. 101:3-8).

A false witness will not go unpunished and he who pours out lies will not go free (Prov. 19:5).

A false witness will not go unpunished and he who pours out lies will perish (Prov. 19:9)

"But the things that come out of the mouth come from the heart and these make a man unclean. For out of the heart come evil thoughts, murder, adultery, sexual immorality, theft, false testimony, slander" (Matt. 15:18-19).

How serious is wearing the belt of truth? As Christians we cannot lie, stretch, or twist the truth. If someone chooses to falsely accuse us or paint us as a liar, remember that they are using the dream labels of the devil and those labels will never stick. When we realize the grave truth that is repeated throughout Scripture, that these people will not receive a standing before the Lord and that their actions against us will cause them to perish for all eternity, our hearts change. It is only then that we can truly understand Christ's advice to us in Matthew 5: 43-45:

"You have heard that it was said, 'Love your neighbor and hate your enemy.' But I tell you: Love your enemies and pray for those who persecute you, that you may be sons of your

Father in heaven. He causes his sun to rise on the evil and the good, and sends rain on the righteous and the unrighteous."

When you grasp the truth from the Word of God that those people who are causing you great pain are on their way to an eternal hell, don't you want to pray for them? Can you drop to your knees fast enough? Yours prayers may be the only prayers anyone ever whispers into your Heavenly Father's ears on their behalf, and that is the truth. This is the full armor of God in action, truth observed and embraced, shooting prayers directly toward the hearts and lives of the enemy troops.

If Satan applies the dream label of "liar" on your life and you pray for the Holy Spirit of God to save the life of the one Satan is using to attack you, his dream becomes a nightmare. For when you love with the love of God and you know the truth of Scripture and catapult it into action, Satan will keep his labels off of your life. First Peter 3:9-12 warns:

> Do not repay evil with evil or insult with insult, but with blessing, because to this you were called so that you may inherit a blessing. For who ever would love life and see good days must keep his tongue from evil and his lips from deceitful speech. He must turn from evil and do good: we must seek peace and pursue it. For the eyes of the Lord are on the righteous and his ears are attentive to their prayer, but the face of the Lord is against those who do evil.

Being falsely accused, harassed, or lied about is a terrible ordeal for any human to endure. Yet we need to recognize that this is a frequently utilized tactic that Satan applied to Christ and also to the believers at Pentecost. Remember their label? Acts 2: 13: "Some, however made fun of them and said, 'They have had too much wine.'"

How can we be surprised or distressed when we are falsely accused and labeled by the devil with the titles that he can only dream that we would adhere to? If Christ can endure being called devil-possessed and the believers covered by the Holy Spirit can be labeled as drunks, regardless of the label we receive, it seems we are among the best company. A label or false accusation is merely an attempt by the evil one to attach a lie to someone who is representing truth. Lies are like mudslinging. In the event someone slings mud at you, remember you are simply a Christian covered with mud. A shower can remove the mess, but mud slinging can never remove your Christianity. Mud can't go that deep!

Enemy Tactic 4: "You don't need to go to church. You can worship God on your own!"

I recently cared for a 92-year-old woman who was confused, manipulative, and obstinate. She would not listen to the staff and would climb out of bed with great agility even though she was unable to walk. She would make it to her wheelchair in seconds and move her feet faster than Fred Flintstone. She could motor all around her room or out in the hall, wherever she set her mind to go. She was a great fall risk. She was searching desperately for her son, John. The hospital operator called to inform me that this patient repeatedly was soliciting the operator for help in calling her son. She wanted her son to come and take her home. The only information she gave the operator was that her son was John. She was so distraught, I gave him a call.

John is 72 years old. I had met him the day before and when he was in her room she was a totally different person. Twenty minutes after I our phone conversation, here came John walking down the hall, his hands in the pockets of his gray jacket, shaking his head with a half smile, half frown on his face. I approached him and apologized for calling him on Saturday morning. I explained what a difficult time his mother was having without him.

Once John entered the room, this lady smiled and proceeded to go right to sleep for about two hours.

I completed my duties and gave medications to my four other patients, then I bought John a cup of coffee, and we sat and talked quietly on the couch while his mother snored away. John told me all about his life.

John explained that his father was a minister and was responsible for his mother's behavior. His dad married her at 20 and placed her on a pedestal. He preached back in the days when preachers were not compensated financially, so he had a job as a carpenter. He was a big man with huge muscular arms, and he would work all day, come home every night, cook supper, clean house, and do the laundry. In the mornings he would get all the kids ready for school, and his wife never did anything. He did it all. John informed me that his mother's behavior was intentional, manipulative, and that she had been selfish all her life. He explained that he was quite sure she was just as manipulative now despite her dementia.

Then the subject matter changed. I told John that I was in the process of writing a Christian book and was working on a chapter about the tactics of the devil. I asked him if he could provide me with any of his thoughts on Satan's ways. John shared the following personal story that hopefully will benefit many.

Poor Judgment

My dad was a very devoted man of God. He fasted and prayed every Monday, Wednesday, and Friday. He raised all of us kids in the Lord. We knew our Bible, and we never missed church.

When I was in my thirties, I was at church one day and I looked around at some of the church people and I began to judge them. They were nothing but a bunch of hypocrites. I made the decision right then that I didn't need to be going to church exposing my family to such, so we stopped going to church altogether. I was confident that I could worship God on my own. I didn't need the church. I knew my Bible, and I was confident that I could raise my children as Christians. It wasn't long after I quit attending church that I started to smoke cigarettes. Then I took up social drinking. Then I became an alcoholic. I woke up one day and realized that I was also a drug addict. I was addicted to prescription drugs given to me by various physicians.

I had a talk with my children. I wasn't about to be a hypocrite. So I told them, "I can't preach to you about smoking or drinking because I do it. If you want to smoke and drink, you don't have to sneak around, it's here in the house. Just help yourself."

At this point I asked him, "John, whatever happened that brought you back to God?"

With tears in his eyes he replied, "I was holding the hand of my daughter when she took her last breath. She died at thirty of alcoholism. When I left her bedside, I ran to the church. I ran to God, I ran for prayer and fellowship and help."

Churches are not filled with perfect people, just forgiven sinners. Remember that Satan can use anyone at anytime. People in the church can aggravate and frustrate one another. We need to realize that it is not our place to weigh and measure the lives of others. That job belongs to Jesus Christ, not you or me. We are there to worship and praise our God. We are there to learn His Word. We are there to encourage, edify, and esteem one another as valuable and precious. We need to help each other be accountable to God's expectations, not man's judgments. It is God we need to please.

Separation from the body of Christ is a common tactic that Satan uses often. This past year, I cared for a man who was recovering from open-heart surgery. I was his primary nurse for three consecutive twelve-hour shifts. The first day the subject of faith came up, and the patient made this comment, "I don't have any faith. I have lost my faith."

My response to him was, "That's okay. Maybe I can help you find it!"

As the weekend continued, he disclosed to me that he had left his faith and his church. He could not bear the sex scandals that had surfaced. He was ashamed of all the priests who had been involved with so many children that he made the decision to leave his faith and his church.

I reminded him of a very important fact. "Men did those things, not God."

We should never stop loving or worshipping God because men misrepresent him from the pew or the pulpit. Yet Satan knows that if he can keep people from the church, there goes fellowship, support, encouragement, and godly education. Satan prefers our ignorance and non-participation. When a person feels as though he can worship God on Sunday mornings by fishing or riding motorcycles or any other activity that takes the place of church and Sunday school, he is falling for another lie. The common excuse of "Sunday is the only morning I get to sleep in!" is truly a cop-out, because many churches now have a variety of services from Saturday evening through Sunday. If you think that you can worship God on your own, and that you don't need to attend church, please remember John's story. It's a lie; he lived it and shared the outcome with you so that you don't fall for enemy Tactic 4.

The next enemy tactic is one that I personally detest.

Enemy Tactic 5: "Your sin is greater than the cross."

Satan's goal is to prevent as many people as possible from accepting Christianity. He loves to negate the power of the cross and block the forgiveness of sin by swelling up the sins within the heart of man. He tells some that there is nothing that can be done to erase wrongs. He tells people over and over that they are not worthy of Christ. There are Christians who have experienced a close relationship with Christ at some point in their lives and then, just as David, they began to climb Satan's ladder of evil ways. When the ladder collapses beneath them, they don't ever recuperate from their fall. They don't ever get up again. Satan fills their minds with tremendous doses of shame, guilt, and the continual playing of reruns of their sinful ways. He keeps these Christians down by affirming their backslidden condition.

"You knew better, and you did it anyway."

"You don't deserve to say His name, let alone call yourself His."

"Your sin is greater than grace. You sinned willingly, knowingly, and unashamedly."

"You can never be forgiven, so don't bother asking."

"Forgiveness is not available to you. You had it, you lost it, and you are most unworthy."

When the devil convinces a person that his or her sins are greater than the forgiveness of Christ, what exactly is he saying? Satan is doing what he has always done. He is accusing Jesus Christ of lying.

In John 1:29, John the Baptist saw Jesus coming toward him and said, "Look the Lamb of God, who takes away the sin of the world."

Isaiah 1:18 writes, "'Come let us reason together,' says the Lord. 'Though your sins be as scarlet, they shall be as white as snow, though they are red as crimson they will be as wool.'"

Romans 10:9-10 promises us, "If you confess with your mouth, Jesus is Lord, and believe in your heart that God raised him from the dead you will be saved. For it is with your heart that you believe and are justified and it is with your mouth that you confess and are saved."

So Satan resurrects your sinful condition and convinces you that your sins were never included in any washing and that you are essentially doomed. He wants you to look Christ square in the eye and shout, "Come down from that cross. What you suffered wasn't enough to cover my sin. Let me hang there instead. My sins are too great, and your death was for everyone but me."

Clinging to thoughts such as these enables the enemy to once again instill deliberate lies intended to negate the very power of the cross of Calvary. This weapon of deadly despair is quite successful, for once this twisted thought pattern is accepted, these dear people feel so unworthy that they won't confess their sin. Some people even convince themselves that, since they are not sincerely sorry for their sin, they can't repent. So they don't.

We all have sinned and fallen short of the glory of God. This is Scripture. But as we have already established, lost ones cannot hear or understand God's Word or His meaning. *When Satan prevents sinful man from confession, repentance, and acceptance of forgiveness by persuading him or her that there is no redemption available for their sins, he keeps a nonbeliever a nonbeliever.* If he can tempt believers into sin and then convince them not to ask for or accept forgiveness, he is causing great damage to the body of Christ.

Examine this tactic with serious concentration and understanding as I try to unveil this horrendous lie. If you believe this lie, that your sin is greater than the cross of Jesus, can you contemplate the message that you are sending to the Almighty God?

God, I know that you sent your son to die for my sins on the cross. He supposedly took all my sin but that is a lie. You see, God, my sin is beyond any forgiveness you could ever attempt to send my way. I can't confess or repent because no one can take away my sin or forgive me, let alone give me righteousness or peace. *I won't let You!* If I can't forgive myself, how in the world could You ever expect me to accept Your forgiveness? I'm unworthy. I am not sorry for the choices I have made in my life. If I had it to live over again, I wouldn't change a thing. I'm going to hell and I know it. So, I will die in my sin, and I will die without You. Jesus Christ is not powerful enough to deal with the enormity of *my* sin. Thanks, but no thanks.

'Sin'-cerely,

A lost soul who is satisfied with a Satan-sealed, sin-saturated, self-martyrdom complex

Do you understand how Satan can come up with such ideas to plant into people's minds? Well think about this. Can Satan and his demons ever be forgiven for their mutiny? *No!* Are their sins beyond forgiveness? *Yes!* Are they doomed to hell and know it? *Absolutely!* When Satan plants Tactic 5 firmly into your heart and mind, and convinces you that it is true, he is extending his wicked hand to grab onto yours and quickly pull you into the muck and mire from which he and his fallen angels can never escape.

But it's not true. It is such a lie. Forgiveness is available to any human being who chooses to confess and repent of the sin in their lives. Men and women can be forgiven regardless of what they have done. God forgives and He forgets and there is no sin that He cannot remove. You can never believe that the power of the cross of Jesus Christ can be diminished or negated by any such thought. Purposely place your sin in proper standing at the foot of the cross, and the precious blood of Christ will remove your sin from your life and from God's memory bank. We stand before Him with our sins in our hands and say, "Lord I am so sorry for hurting You. Please forgive me of my sins." And He responds, "What sins?"

Whenever a person totally understands the power of the cross of Christ, the only response that validates God's plan is this one word: *gone!* Your sins are gone. It is only when we live believing that our sins are *no more* that we have any right to call ourselves Christians. We were purchased with a price, and we have great value to God. Is it any wonder that Satan would want to keep us bound and dead in our sin? I believe that of all the enemy tactics, this one must pain or anger Christ more than any other. Don't believe this deadly lie. Confess your sins, turn away from your life of self, and turn to God. Then you can live with the undeniable confidence that your sins are forgiven and gone—forever. No one who ever lived on this earth has ever done any thing so despicable that Calvary could not cleanse. There is *no* sin greater than the cross, no not one.

Enemy Tactic 6: "You can be God!"

In the garden, Satan nudged Adam and Eve to take and eat the forbidden fruit from the tree of the Knowledge of Good and Evil. He pressed them and tempted them with the thought that "you too can be like God." Today Satan simply convinces people that they can be their own god. Each one can control his destiny and be in charge of his own life with no fear of social or moral punishment or interventions. So the determination of what is right or wrong is completely in the hands of each individual. There is no standard, no judgment, and no "forbidden fruit." Humanism is the term used to describe this concept. Relinquishing control to God is the very struggle many people have in coming to Christ. One good friend of mine describes her perceptions of the Christian life before she became a believer.

Christians are stereotyped by the world as freaky, emotionally constipated, personality types. Often viewed as fun-haters, prudish, and boring, who would relish the thought of being a freak or a prude? Resigning status as god of her own life, she considered all the great things she loved to do and felt that Christianity would put a halt to passion and excitement. She truly thought the cost of Christianity was more than she was willing to pay. She understands a person not wanting to give up control.

When people adopt the belief that they can be god of their own life, it isn't easy to relinquish the throne. Yet when we stop trying to be someone we are not, accept who we are, and weigh our losses and our gains, we have to laugh at ourselves. The gains of Christianity can never compare to the things we once listed as losses. When we were lost, we did not realize the gains: peace of knowing without a doubt that we could be saved from hell, loved by God, and promised eternal life. First John 5:13 is one of the most compelling scriptures to place in your heart and memory bank: "I write these things to you who believe in the name of the Son of God so that you may *know* that you have eternal life" (*italics* added). Eternal life is a definite gain.

Satan loves to twist the truth. He wants us to believe that the personal cost of Christianity is much too great for an individual to bear? Christ paid it all. The cost of Christianity to anyone is free. It cost Christ his life so that we gain access to God.

Satan also loves to promote the concept that you can't be a Christian because you have too much to lose. Satan has such a great way of twiddling with truth. A sinner does have a lot to lose: a lot of sin, pain, shame, regret, ignorance, and uncertainty.

A necessary step in the consideration of becoming a Christian is accepting this fact: you are not God. You are a forgiven sinner with lots to lose and more to gain. You cannot replace the Most High. After you know Him, you will gladly take your seat on the floor beside His feet as He sits and reigns from His proper seat. Isaiah 46: 8-9, clearly denounces Satan's tactic 6: "*Remember this, fix it in mind, take it to heart, you rebels. Remember the former things, those of long ago; I am God and there is no other; I am God, and there is none like me*" (*italics* added).

The six enemy tactics identified in this chapter are serious and potentially dangerous to the believer and non-believer. Review the list of lies:

1. "There is no such place as Hell? The devil does not exist! There will never be a Judgment Day!"
2. Climb up the ladder of rationalization in order to justify your evil ways.
3. Satan's dream labels of false accusation and harassment produce permanent damage to an innocent person's reputation.
4. "You don't need to go to church. You can worship God on your own."

5. "Your sin is greater than the cross."
6. "You can be God."

We have evaluated some of the methods and strategies of Satan in order to be better prepared to protect ourselves. The knowledge that he can have us in his sights at anytime is incentive for us to take cover. Our cover is the full armor of God. Daily we must carefully and consistently hold to all God has given us. We must trust in His power, His command, and victoriously live our lives knowing Satan exists. Hell is real. Judgment Day is coming. Lies cannot be rationalized. Evil labels will never stick or leave any mark on anyone covered with God's gear. We need church and fellowship. One person does not make up the body of Christ: we need all the members. Cling to the truth that there is no sin greater than the Cross. God is God. Keep him on His throne. God and only God has all the power we will ever need to stand firm against the enemy's tactics, as illustrated so eloquently in the following Psalms:

> As for God, his way is perfect;
>   the word of the Lord is flawless.
> He is a shield
>   for all who take refuge in him.
> For who is God besides the Lord?
>   And who is the Rock except our God?
> It is God who arms me with strength
>   and makes my way perfect.
> He makes my feel like the feet of a deer;
>   he enables me to stand on the heights.
> He trains my hands for battle;
>   my arms can bend a bow of bronze.
> You give me your shield of victory,
>   and your right hand sustains me;
>   you stoop down to make me great.
> You broaden the path beneath me,
>   so that my ankles do not turn.
> I pursued my enemies and overtook them;

I did not turn back until they were destroyed.
I crushed them so they could not rise;
   they fell beneath my feet.
You armed me with strength for battle;
   you made my adversaries bow at my feet (Ps. 18:30-39).

The Lord lives! Praise be to my Rock!
   Exalted be God my Savior!
He is the God who avenges me,
   who subdues nations under me,
   who saves me from my enemies (Ps. 18:46-48).

9. Are You Looking for a Sign?

JOHNNY WAS ONLY TWENTY-FOUR years old and had suffered for such a long time. Cancer had eaten away at the left side of his face and jaw, and he was heavily sedated because the pain was excruciating. He had put up such a fight, and his struggle was soon to be over.

Johnny's loving and supportive family, stayed at the hospital night and day. They were people of prayer and great faith and were so eager for his suffering to cease. Not feeling the need to be in the room when he passed away, they went to get some sleep in the waiting room. They knew the nursing staff would be with him through the night. Tight bonds of love develop between nurses, patients, and families in intensive care units. Whenever a patient spends his last moments on this earth in a hospital setting, he is seldom alone. Nurses have a tendency to draw near. One nurse was holding Johnny's hand and quietly talking to this dear young man, as we all watched the EKG monitor above his bed. His heart rate began to slow severely, and it wasn't long before his heart gave up the battle and a flat line appeared.

The very moment Johnny crossed over to eternity, the windows of the hospital room flew open. Wide-eyed and covered with shock and fear, we nurses looked at one another in amazement. This room was located in the older portion of the hospital. The architecture was gothic stone and the windows were framed in black wrought iron. Not one of us had any idea that these windows could even open. Our minds began to try to find a logical explanation for this happening. We thought that perhaps a change in barometric pressure, a southern storm squall, a tornado, or some other weather event caused the windows to burst open. But the windows opened to a lighted courtyard, and in the midst of the yard there stood a beautiful tree. Not one leaf of that tree stirred. There was an eerie stillness in the dark of the early morning. It happened to be Easter.

We gathered our wits about us and made our way to the visitors' lounge to awaken the mother and sister. Once they were awake, I quietly relayed the anticipated news "Your prayers are answered," I said. "Your son's suffering is over. It's Easter morning, and your son and brother is spending it in heaven."

Without any hesitation whatsoever, the mother grabbed a hold of my arm and with a tremendous degree of expectation and wonder she asked me this question "Was there a sign? We've been praying for a sign! Was there a sign?"

I looked at my co-workers and with tears in our eyes, I answered her question.

"Oh, boy! Do I have a sign for you!"

I have always treasured the memory of that Easter. I haven't any idea what the significance of this mother's sign was to indicate however, I will never forget her faith.

She had asked God to do something extraordinary, and He did. She was anticipating, watching, and waiting.

Scripture is full of signs, miracles, and wonders as well as prophecies fulfilled and promises delivered. Signs of Jesus' first and second coming should give us hope and fill our hearts with great expectation and anticipation. In this chapter, let us remember the people and events that lead to a promised Savior. Think about the faithful ones who spent their lives waiting to see the Messiah. What source of power did these dear ones cling to that prevented them from ever giving up hope of the One who was promised? Dare we who claim Christ in our lives today live with such an expectation? He is coming again. Are we looking for a sign?

Signs of a Savior

In Isaiah 7: 10–14, the Prophet told Ahaz to ask the Lord your God for a sign, whither in the deepest depths or in the highest heights. Ahaz refused so Isaiah said:

"Hear now, you house of David! Is it not enough to try the patience of men? Will you try the patience of God also? Therefore the *Lord himself will give you a sign;* The virgin will be with child and will give birth to a son and will call him Immauel" (*italics* added).

This is the familiar story of the promised Messiah, who was to be born of Mary and God's Holy Spirit. Another sign appeared in the sky and Magi were watching.

"After Jesus was born in Bethlehem in Judea, during the time of King Herod, Magi from the east came to Jerusalem and asked, 'Where is the one who has been born King of the Jews? We saw His star in the East and have come to worship him.'" (Matt. 2:1-2).

The star was a sign and it spurred the Magi into action. They went looking for Jesus and found him. The shepherds had done so earlier.

And there were shepherds living out in the fields nearby, keeping watch over their flocks at night. An angel of the Lord appeared to them, and the glory of the Lord shown around them, and they were terrified. But the angels said to them, "Do not be afraid. I bring you good news of great joy that will be for all people. Today in the town of David a Savior has been born to you: He is Christ the Lord. This will be a *sign* to you: You will find a baby wrapped in cloths and lying in a manger" (Luke 2:8-2, *italics* added).

So they hurried off and found Mary and Joseph and the baby who was lying in the manger (Luke 2:16).

The shepherds returned, glorifying and praising God for all the things they had heard and seen, which were just as they had been told (Luke 2:20).

After they heard the King, they went on their way, and the star they had seen in the east went ahead of them until it stopped over the place where the child was. When they saw the star they were overjoyed. On coming to the house, they saw the child with his mother Mary, and they bowed down and worshiped him. Then they opened their treasures and presented him with gifts of gold and of incense and of myrrh (Matt. 2:9-11).

Remember Simeon and Anna?

Now there was a man in Jerusalem called Simeon, who was righteous and devout. He was waiting for the consolation of Israel and the Holy Spirit was upon him. It had been revealed to him by the Holy Spirit that he would not die before he had seen the Lord's Christ. Moved by the Spirit, he went into the temple courts. When the parents brought in the child Jesus to do for him what the custom of the Law required, Simeon took him in his arms and praised God, saying:

"Sovereign Lord, as you have promised, you now dismiss your servant in peace. For my eyes have seen your salvation, which you have prepared in the sight of all people, a light for revelation to the Gentiles and for glory to your people Israel."

The child's father and mother marveled at what was said about him. Then Simeon blessed them and said to Mary, his mother. "This child is destined to cause the falling and rising of many in Israel and to be a *sign* that will be spoken against, so that the thoughts of many hearts will be revealed and a sword will pierce your own soul too" (Luke 2: 25-35, *italics* added).

There was also a prophetess, Anna, the daughter of Phanuel, of the tribe of Asher. She was very old; she had lived with her husband seven years after her marriage, and then was a widow until she was eighty-four. She never left the temple but worshiped night and day, fasting and praying. Coming up to them at that very moment, she gave thanks to God and spoke about the child to all who were looking forward to the redemption of Jerusalem (Luke 2: 36-38).

These above excerpts make some excellent points. Signs were available, and some people saw the signs, investigated them for significance, and were more than willing to follow whatever path the signs led them to take. Those who were open to believe were from all walks of life. So it is with the coming of our Lord today. Some want to be prepared and acknowledge that signs are of value and that we need to review them often and hold them near to our hearts. Signs of the second coming of Christ are also filled with warning signals and serious messages that stress the importance of readiness.

I hope that we are ready and that our responses will be appropriate. But there is a chance that some of us may ignore the warnings. Let me share a recent event that will illustrate how easy it is to be complacent when blaring signals warn of certain disaster. This is quite an embarrassing moment for me to share, but if it helps just one other person to safety, I'll endure it!

Our nation has experienced many disasters in recent years. There is a severe weather warning system close to my home, and the siren kept blasting through the wee hours of the morning. When my husband got up and looked out the window, he saw severe lightning, but the wind wasn't blowing. We didn't turn on the news or investigate further. We just went back to sleep. The next morning we found out that an F3 tornado had hit a trailer court and several homes less than fifteen miles from our home. Loss of life was great for people were asleep in their beds.

We had heard the sirens. There had to be significant signs of dangerous weather for the warning to go on for so long, but we did not heed it. We didn't investigate the possibility that there was a significant storm system brewing. We thought thunderstorm, not deadly tornado.

Do you think that the next time the sirens go off that we will stay in bed? No way. We will do a thorough investigation and secure as many lives as possible. Many friends and family members are beyond earshot of the sirens. If a "next time" arises we will be notifying our loved ones instead of covering up and going back to sleep. We will be awake.

We need to be on the same alert for the signs of Jesus' second coming. Are we heeding the indicators from Christ that he clearly stated would be present prior to His appearing? Review the following passages that deal with this subject matter. Are we looking for a sign? Can we identify a sign when we see one? Are we prepared? Are we going to heed any warning that Jesus gives?

"At the time the kingdom of heaven will be like ten virgins who took their lamps and went out to meet the bridegroom. Five of them were foolish and five were wise. The foolish ones took their lamps but did not take any oil with them. The wise, however, took oil in jars along with their lamps. The bridegroom was a long time in coming, and they all became drowsy and fell asleep. At midnight the cry rang out: 'Here's the bridegroom! Come out to meet him!'

"Then all the virgins woke up and trimmed their lamps. The foolish ones said to the wise, 'Give us some of your oil; our lamps are going out.'

"'No,' they replied, 'there may not be enough for both us and you. Instead, go to those who sell oil and buy some for yourselves.'

"But while they were on their way to buy the oil, the bridegroom arrived. The virgins who were ready went in with him to the wedding banquet. And the door was shut. Later the others also came. 'Sir! Sir!' they said. 'Open the door for us!'

"But he replied, 'I tell you the truth, I don't know you.'

"Therefore keep watch, because you do not know the day or the hour" (Matt. 25:1-13).

Don't you want to be among the wise in the event that Christ comes in the middle of the night? The above passage makes it clear that we should not wait until the last moment to establish a relationship with the bridegroom. Knowing someone well requires spending time together. Loving someone well means that there is a commitment that exceeds emotion. We need that kind of closeness with Christ before the day that He arrives. Then that day will be a glorious mountaintop adventure that we have been expecting to enjoy.

That passage and many others repeatedly state that the actual date, hour, or season is not going to be revealed. God has not given us an exact time. We cannot schedule the second coming of Christ in our day planners or on our calendars. However, just because we are ignorant of the date does not exempt us from processing the data that Christ did report to us all.

> "Now learn this lesson from the fig tree: As soon as its twigs get tender and its leaves come out, you know that summer is near. Even so, when you see all these things, you know that it is near, right at the door. I tell you the truth, this generation will certainly not pass away until these things have happened. Heaven and earth will pass away but my words will never pass away."
>
> "No one knows about that day or hour, not even the angels in heaven, nor the Son, but only the Father. As it was in the days of Noah, so it will be at the coming of the Son of Man. For in the days before the flood, people were eating and drinking, marrying and giving in marriage, up to the day Noah entered the ark and they knew nothing about what would happen until the flood came and took them all away. That is how it will be at the coming of the Son of Man" (Matt. 24:32-39).

Can you imagine the enormity of the flood that overtook the people on the earth in Noah's day? Since we have experienced the tsunami and the hurricanes that brought floods to various areas of the United States in recent years, we can read this passage with a greater degree of understanding. What once seemed to be so far from our imagination has become real. We have seen images of flooding, disaster, and loss of life. The earthquake in Pakistan and the tornado previously mentioned in my hometown have provided the world with persistently blaring wake-up calls. We are becoming quite familiar with situations that are out of our control. Here today and gone tomorrow. We are seeing families and neighborhoods obliterated from this earth. Are we prepared to step into eternity?

> "Therefore keep watch, because you do not know on what

day your Lord will come. But understand this: If the owner of the house had known at what time of night the thief was coming he would have kept watch and would not have let his house be broken into. So you also must be ready, because the Son of Man will come at an hour when you do not expect him" (Matt. 24:42-44).

So what will be happening in society and in our world in the last days? Second Timothy 3:1-4 gives us an idea of people's behavior and actions:

"But mark this: There will be terrible times in the last days. People will be lovers of themselves, lovers of money, boastful, proud, abusive, disobedient to parents, ungrateful, unholy, without love, unforgiving, slanderous, without self-control, brutal, not lovers of good, treacherous, rash, conceited, lovers of pleasure rather than lovers of God."

Watching, waiting, and knowing that Jesus will arrive one day when we least expect Him. Have you ever watched and waited for something or someone? Well, I confess that I do quite often. One week this past fall, the weather was absolutely beautiful. It was seventy degrees and the sun was shining, the leaves were falling, and my lantana and morning glories were still brilliant with their deep purple, orange, yellow, and red blossoms.

I jumped into my favorite clothes—jeans, sweatshirt and sneakers—and headed for the little shed in the backyard. I was on a mission to clean with fury. I filled the metal bucket with a bleach solution and mild detergent and gathered up my brushes and turned on the hose. I spent the entire morning in a scrubbing frenzy, and I cleaned my bird feeders, birdbaths, and birdseed containers. I am a birder, I confess!

Everything clean and drying in the sunshine, I hopped in the car and went to get fresh seed, peanuts, and suet. I usually feed my birds year round. In the spring I put out suet for it is soft and easy for the mother birds to feed their wee ones. I have had the joy to see so many different babies. My mocking bird had twins one year and they preferred the orange suet. I believe that every type of woodpecker family has spent time in my backyard. Last spring was extremely special for me when a huge pileated mom and dad came to feed their youngster. They preferred the peanut suet, and that baby was the biggest baby bird I have ever laid my eyes on. You cannot believe the beauty of those red, black, and white birds flying all around my backyard. A pair of red-breasted grosbeaks makes an annual visit to my feeders each spring. The couple is probably on their way up north but they stay and eat for about four weeks. I love to see them come to my feeder. I have an indigo bunting, and this year he ate thistle from the thistle bag with about eighteen goldfinches. That truly was a display of pure color—the yellow and black birds and one lovely blue guy all hanging on that white sock bag!

I spend a lot of time watching and waiting to see what birds God may send into my yard. Once he sent a wild monk parakeet so lime green that I thought I was hallucinating. He sent me a sharp-shinned hawk that was unbelievably big, but I'm glad he didn't hang around long. One of my favorite bird-watching moments happened recently. I was sitting on my yard swing and praying as I watched the beautiful goldfinches. All of a sudden I heard a noise in the holly tree behind me, and when I turned around I was overwhelmed. There was a flock of the most beautiful birds I have only seen in my bird books. There must have been twenty or thirty cedar waxwings feasting on my holly berries. What a blessing to me. I was amazed. They stripped every berry off of that tree within four hours time, and I haven't seen them since!

Now that you know I am a "watcher," let me take you back to my initial story. When I returned home with all of my brand new seed, I filled my feeders. I kept watching. The birds didn't come. I had been on vacation and had neglected to feed and water them. It had been a great year for the birds for there was plenty of natural food sources and they did not need to rely on feeding stations as much. I was so disappointed. I had everything ready, but they didn't come.

When I think about signs of the times, I can't help but think of our Heavenly Father. His feeding stations are always clean, purified, sanctified, and spotless. He never neglects His part. He provides us with Living Water, and the Bread of Life and tells us to taste and see that the Lord is good. He watches and waits for us to come. I can imagine only a sliver of the joy that He must experience each time someone shows

up at His feeding station. We need to come to Him, before He comes
to us. Don't disappoint Him. Don't keep Him waiting. The signs are
serious, and they seem very near.

> Fly to him with utmost haste.
> You have no time to waste.
> Before him bow
> The time is now
> Eternity awaits.

Are you looking forward to eternity? Are you aware that the Lord
has a display of His most precious jewels waiting for us to enjoy? His
description of the New Jerusalem is covered with beauty. Remember that
our life with Christ does not end when we enter heaven. We continue
on an adventure that is everlasting. We need to keep on looking forward
to the unending creativity and preparations that He is constantly making for us. Enjoy His display as I leave you to wander through His
glory found in Revelation 21:9-27.

> One of the seven angels who had the seven bowls full of the
> seven last plagues came and said to me, "Come, I will show
> you the bride, the wife of the Lamb." And he carried me away
> in the Spirit to a mountain great and high, and showed me the
> Holy City, Jerusalem, coming down out of heaven from God.
> It shone with the glory of God, and its brilliance was like that
> of a very precious jewel, like a jasper, clear as crystal. It had a
> great, high wall with twelve gates, and with twelve angels at
> the gates. On the gates were written the names of the twelve
> tribes of Israel. There were three gates on the east, three on
> the north, three on the south and three on the west. The wall
> of the city had twelve foundations, and on them were the
> names of the twelve apostles of the Lamb.
> The angel who talked with me had a measuring rod of gold
> to measure the city, its gates and its walls. The city was laid
> out like a square, as long as it was wide. He measured the city
> with the rod and found it to be 12,000 stadia in length, and as

wide and high as it is long. He measured its wall and it was 144 cubits thick, by man's measurement, which the angel was using. The wall was made of jasper, and the city of pure gold, as pure as glass. The foundations of the city walls were decorated with every kind of precious stone. The first foundation was jasper, the second sapphire, the third chalcedony, the fourth emerald, the fifth sardonyx, the sixth carnelian, the seventh chrysolite, the eighth beryl, the ninth topaz, the tenth chrysoprase, the eleventh jacinth, and the twelfth amethyst. The twelve gates were twelve pearls, each gate made of a single pearl. The great street of the city was of pure gold, like transparent glass.

I did not see a temple in the city, because the Lord God Almighty and the Lamb are its temple. The city does not need the sun or the moon to shine on it, for the glory of God gives it light, and the Lamb is its lamp. The nations will walk by its light, and the kings of the earth will bring their splendor into it. On no day will its gates ever be shut, for there will be no night there. The glory and honor of the nations will be brought into it. Nothing impure will ever enter it, nor will anyone who does what is shameful or deceitful but only those whose names are written in the Lamb's book of life.

Conclusion

HAVE YOU DISCOVERED some piece from this collection that delivers healing in your life? Private collections of His presence in our lives will grow as long as we live. God's critical care continues. This book has come to a close, and you must find a place for it on a shelf in your home. Then again, maybe it isn't meant to be shelved, but placed gently into the hands of someone you know who may be in search of a gem from God.

I would like very much to pray with you before I leave you. Please come with me to our Father's throne.

Precious Lord Most High,
We bow before You in humility knowing that we have all fallen short of Your glory. Forgive us, dear Father, if we have done anything to break Your heart. We believe in you Lord. We believe in Your Word as truth. We believe in Your Son, Jesus Christ and in Your precious Holy Spirit, our Companion and our Comforter.

Lord, please hear our hearts and our requests as we place them at your feet. Never let us take our "Slice of Salvation" for granted. Take us from the point of *believing in you* to the real heart of Christianity that is: *knowing you.*

As you orchestrate our lives and circumstances by blessing us with the "rest of the story," help us to continually stand in awe of Your handiwork and creativity.

Keep us connected to You daily, with a quality prayer life. Help us to enjoy the privilege of Your accessibility. Make us better listeners wanting to hear You now and always.

Please help us to review and remember Your amazing promises. Thank You for being Truth. Let us accept our responsibilities to find and meet Your expectations, whole-heartedly. Help us to do what You command with willingness and a great desire to please only You.

When it comes to pain and loss, draw ever near to all of us. We know that we are not exempt, and we also know that You are familiar with grief and sorrow. Keep our eyes fixed upon You and not the circumstances. Let us always be aware of Your presence whenever the pain seems like more than we can bear. Draw near, come close, and stay awhile. May we always need You and never let us push You away.

Father, the enemy is raging. Thank You for your Class "A" dress-suit of body armor. Keep us covered. Keep us safe. Make us consistent for we never want to be vulnerable. Give us discipline in prayer, Your Word, in thoughts, in knowing and spreading Your good news.

Father, also for those in our lives who have fallen for the lies of the enemy, please dispatch Your Spirit. Remove the blinders from their eyes and penetrate the barriers of rebellion. Each one of us has friends and family Lord, who believe Satan's lies. Please bring them to our side. We want their names written in the Lamb's Book of Life, just as you do. Use any one of us to deliver them. We love the lost in our lives Lord. We pray in earnest Father. Please help us to help You with whatever counter-attack You have planned. We stand with open hands awaiting Your orders.

Signs, Father, we see signs. We are looking for You. Don't ever let complacency overtake us, Lord. Keep us alert, awake, and watching for You to appear. Let our lives exude anticipation and our attitudes overflow with great expectation. Oh Father, find us ready, with oil in our lamps and commitment in our hearts. You have told us repeatedly that You are coming soon. Precious Lord, there will be so many that will be watching and waiting to welcome You. I pray that we increase that number by our lives and our endeavors. In unison of heart we say, "Come Lord Jesus, Come."

Amen.

I Never Walk the Halls Alone
Order Form

Online orders: www.walkthehalls.com

Please send *I Never Walk the Halls Alone* **to:**

Name: _____

Address: _____

City: _____ State: _____

Zip: _____

Telephone: (_____) _____

Book Price: $18.95

Shipping: $3.00 for the first book and $1.00 for each additional book to cover shipping and handling within US, Canada, and Mexico. International orders add $6.00 for the first book and $2.00 for each additional book.

Or order from:
ACW Press
P.O. Box 110390
Nashville, TN 37222

(800) 931-BOOK

or contact your local bookstore